New Sel

VERNON WATKINS was born or
Wales. He lived most of his li
his wife and five children, and
clerk for Lloyds Bank. During his litetime six volumes of his poetry
were published by Faber & Faber, with a seventh appearing
posthumously. At his death he had won several major poetry
prizes, was a visiting Professor of Poetry in America, and was being
considered for Poet Laureate. He was friends with poets as diverse
as: W.B. Yeats, T.S. Eliot, David Jones, Dylan Thomas, Philip
Larkin, R.S. Thomas and Kathleen Raine, who considered him 'the
greatest lyric poet of my generation'. Vernon Watkins died in
America on 8 October 1967.

RICHARD RAMSBOTHAM was born in Northumberland in 1962. He
read English at Cambridge, and lectured in English at Warsaw
University from 1989 to 1993. He teaches Speech and Drama for a
living. He is the author of *Who Wrote Bacon? William Shakespeare,
Francis Bacon and James I: A Mystery for the Twenty-First Century*
(Temple Lodge, 2004), and is currently writing the authorised
biography of Vernon Watkins.

Fyfield*Books* aim to make available some of the great classics of British and European literature in clear, affordable formats, and to restore often neglected writers to their place in literary tradition.

Fyfield*Books* take their name from the Fyfield elm in Matthew Arnold's 'Scholar Gypsy' and 'Thyrsis'. The tree stood not far from the village where the series was originally devised in 1971.

> *Roam on! The light we sought is shining still.*
> *Dost thou ask proof? Our tree yet crowns the hill,*
> *Our Scholar travels yet the loved hill-side*

from 'Thyrsis'

VERNON WATKINS

New Selected Poems

Edited with an introduction by
RICHARD RAMSBOTHAM

FyfieldBooks

CARCANET

First published in Great Britain in 2006 by
Carcanet Press Limited
Alliance House
Cross Street
Manchester M2 7AQ

A CIP catalogue record for this book is available from the British Library
ISBN 1 85754 847 7
978 1 85754 847 1

The publisher acknowledges financial assistance from Arts Council England

Typeset by XL Publishing Services, Tiverton
Printed and bound in England by SRP Ltd, Exeter

Contents

from *The Ballad of the Mari Lwyd* (1941)

from *The Lady with the Unicorn* (1948)

from *The Death Bell* (1954)

from *Cypress and Acacia* (1959)

from *Affinities* (1962)

from *Fidelities* (1968)

New Selected Poems

from *Uncollected Poems* (1969)

from *The Ballad of the Outer Dark* (1979)

from *The Breaking of the Wave* (1979)

Rarely Published and Unpublished Poems

Contents

Foreword by Rowan Williams, the Archbishop of Canterbury

This volume marks the centenary of the birth of one of the twentieth century's most brilliant and distinctive – and neglected – poets in the English language. As Richard Ramsbotham notes in his penetrating introduction, the reputation of Watkins's friend and fellow-townsman, Dylan Thomas, has overshadowed his own. It is hard to imagine two more different poets – in idiom as much as in lifestyle; but the very fact that they appreciated each other reminds us that there are no textbook requirements for authentic poetry, and that reputations do not have to compete.

Watkins is, on his own account, a 'metaphysical' poet: that is, he aims to make visible something behind the surface of things, like veins standing out in flesh. The image seems appropriate, if only to rebut the charge that he somehow empties out the specificity of landscape or personality in order to evoke timeless patterns. Yet it is impossible to read some of his poems on the Gower peninsula, or the evocations of bird or shell, or the addresses to those he loves and think of these works as abstract. In a very characteristic little poem, 'The Razor Shell' (p.72), we find inseparably bound together the actuality of a physical object and the wild depth of its own hidden inner world. 'Do not interpret me too soon' warns the shell; and the poem is not in that sense interpretation but the large mapping of a context and hinterland still to be explored, felt for, in the poem's words. The poem does not reduce the object to some kind of geometry; it listens for the tides on which the object sails.

These are astonishingly sustained poems. Short or long, they carry their matter forward at a steady pace, with a sense of both verbal and imaginative solidity. Some could be said to have – not a very fashionable thing to ascribe to a poem now, perhaps – a 'liturgical' quality, the effect of a complex ceremony in words. The 'Ballad of the Mari Lwyd', which is, I think, one of his greatest works and one of the outstanding poems of the century, draws together the folk-ritual of the New Year, the Christian Eucharist, the uneasy frontier between living and dead, so as to present a model of what poetry itself is – frontier work between death and life, old year and new, bread and body.

This is an essential collection for all interested in the full, alarming power of poetry. It is a first-class orientation to Watkins's very large corpus of work, and it also, in the aphorisms at the end, directs us towards an authoritative vision of poetic ambition and poetic humility alike. 'A poet need have only one enemy: his reputation.' Watkins's reputation may be overdue for rethinking, but that would be of no great moment in his eyes. He would only ask that we listen with him as well as to him.

+Rowan Cantuar

Introduction

Vernon Watkins was described by Henry Reed in 1945 as 'the one poet of his generation who holds out unequivocal promise of greatness'.[1] Nearly twenty years later, in 1964, Kathleen Raine made it clear that this promise had been fulfilled:

> I first heard the poetry of Vernon Watkins praised in the nineteen thirties, by Dylan Thomas, who then said that he was probably the finest poet then writing in Britain (unless Thomas himself). This was not an obvious judgement at the time... but it is clearly true at the time of writing... because Vernon Watkins has during the intervening years perfected himself in the poetic art as few of his contemporaries have done.[2]

At the time of his death, in 1967, Watkins was one of the clear candidates for Poet Laureate; the previous Laureate, John Masefield, had died on 12 May. Faber, where he was supported by T.S. Eliot, had published six volumes of Watkins's poetry, to increasing acclaim, and had recently brought out his *Selected Poems 1930–1960* (1967); they would shortly bring out his posthumous final collection, *Fidelities*, followed by a memorial volume, *Vernon Watkins 1906–1967*. This included tributes by Michael Hamburger, Ceri Richards and Hugo Williams; elegies by Marianne Moore and R.S. Thomas; an essay by Kathleen Raine, in which she described Watkins as 'the greatest lyric poet of my generation'; and an essay by Philip Larkin, who wrote: 'In Vernon's presence poetry seemed like a living stream, in which one had only to dip the vessel of one's devotion. He made it clear how one could, in fact "live by poetry"; it was a vocation, at once difficult as sainthood and easy as breathing.'

And yet, nearly forty years after his death, Vernon Watkins has disappeared almost completely from the commonly perceived map of twentieth-century poetry. This re-introduction of Watkins, as a poet, will also touch on some of the reasons for such a mysterious vanishing act.

One reason is undoubtedly his own highly unusual attitude to fame and reputation. In countless remarks he reveals that he had no interest whatsoever in acquiring these: 'a poet need have only one enemy: his reputation'; 'a good poem is one which can never be fashionable'; 'publication is a very marginal thing really'.[3] His view is epitomised in 'Rewards of the Fountain':

> Let the world offer what it will,
> Its bargains I refuse.
> Those it rewards are greedy still.
> I serve a stricter Muse.

To gain the right perspective on this, we must know something of Watkins's biography, for this had by no means always been his stance.

Vernon Watkins was born in Maesteg, South Wales, on 27 June 1906. He began writing very young, as he recalled: 'I cannot remember a time when I did not mean to write poetry';[4] or, more exactly, 'I was already writing poems when I was seven or eight, and between that age and twelve I bought the English poets one by one.'[5] He attended Swansea Grammar School for a year, before going to a preparatory school in Sussex and then on to Repton, where he was a contemporary of a very different writer, Christopher Isherwood. (Isherwood portrayed Watkins as Perceval in his fictionalised memoir *Lions and Shadows*.) Watkins went on to Magdalene College, Cambridge, but left after a year, finding it unconducive to the vocation of poetry. Throughout this time, with the exception of his first year at Repton, he had never ceased writing poetry. His ambition and determination to achieve fame as a poet were unambiguous. He later recollected: 'I aimed at writing a kind of poetry that would be remembered after my time';[6] or, more emphatically, 'I wanted, at that early stage, to be "numbered among the English poets".'[7] He had poems published in Cambridge, and one ('True Lovers') in the then prestigious *London Mercury*.

Having left Cambridge, aged nineteen, he returned to Wales and found work as a clerk at Lloyd's Bank in Cardiff. Only once did he refer to this move in writing:

> The relation of a poet to society is something I have never been able to understand or solve. If a poet is able to write plays, that is a help; but, so far, I have not been able to write a play. If he writes criticism, that is a compromise; but I do not write criticism. My whole activity is lyric poetry, which must wait

New Selected Poems

upon itself. When I was eighteen, after writing verse for nine or ten years, I knew that my obsession with poetry disqualified me for anything else. I decided to work in a bank. It happened that I could do figures easily.[8]

The job in the bank was thus the only route Watkins could envisage that would enable him to pursue his poetry without compromise. Dylan Thomas would acknowledge this: 'So many writers, because their own serious writing does not pay, live by writing about writing, lecturing about writing, reviewing other writers, scriptwriting, advertising, journalising, boiling pots for the chainstore publishers; Vernon Watkins writes nothing but poems.'[9]

Initially, though, Watkins's move appeared more like a self-incarceration than a solution: the result was a massive heightening of his inner experience and his poetry, to an extent he was unable to sustain. He spiralled into crisis, in medical terms into a severe psychotic episode, left the bank and Cardiff, and travelled to Repton; there his previous Headmaster, Geoffrey Fisher, the future Archbishop of Canterbury, had him certified and placed in a 'nursing home'. His crisis continued to deepen and transform, leading him eventually 'beyond time's chain',[10] to an inner, spiritual experience or encounter, closely akin to what have since become known as 'near-death experiences'.

He never elaborated on this experience in prose, although he did make several brief allusions to it:

I had read Blake's words:

> Each man is in his Spectre's power
> Until the arrival of that hour
> When his humanity awake
> And cast his spectre into the lake;

And the eternity of which Blake spoke suddenly seemed to me more accessible than time itself.[11]

Elsewhere he said: 'Time itself was changed. It could never again dominate life.'[12]

The experience radically altered Watkins's relationship to his poetry. He destroyed or rejected the vast number of poems he had previously written and started, as it were, afresh. His change was nowhere more apparent than in relation to ambition – to his desire to achieve worldly success as a poet: 'I experienced an upheaval which made my work hitherto worthless, a complete revolution of sensibility. It no longer seemed to me interesting that a poem should be remembered; its sole interest was that it should be valid.'[13] And again: 'The state in which I found myself when I had experienced my metaphysical change was very much like a rebirth. I had died the death of ambition, and found that that death was only a beginning.'[14]

He later offered the following definition: 'A poet is born when his ambition is born; but he is born a metaphysical poet when his ambition dies.'[15]

After an interval Watkins went back to work, at Lloyds Bank in Swansea, where he worked, apart from the War years, until his retirement in 1966. Thus began his solution to the riddle regarding: 'the relation of a poet to society'. As his wife Gwen Watkins put it, 'he worked in the Bank every day and wrote poetry every night'.[16] Watkins himself was able to say: 'If Dante had been a steeplejack and Milton a deep sea diver I can still believe their works would have been written, though not exactly as we have them today... The inevitable part of poetry will always be written. That is why I think a poet can do any work in the world and not lose by it, provided that he is a poet first.'[17]

As a consequence of this resolution, Watkins determined no longer to publish. Eight years later he changed his mind about this, but without altering his new-found attitude to fame and publication. As he wrote to a younger poet in 1941: 'Don't be fascinated by a reputation or the idea of publication; both are a snare for the unwary.'[18]

Watkins's objection to 'reputation' was, primarily, because of its transience. A poet may be 'fashionable' for a while, but unless their work is 'valid' it will have no 'permanence': 'I said to a questioner, If you want a reputation for ten years, put something ingenious into your line; but if you want permanence, for God's sake take it out!'[19] The true artist must therefore meet much greater demands than those that determine public acclaim:

> In every genuine artist the first care is to use his gift in such a way as to satisfy his imaginative need. If the whole world applauds a work, and it does not meet this need, the work, from the point of view of the artist, is a failure. A shallow artist is disheartened by failure, but a profound one is more likely to be disheartened by success.[20]

New Selected Poems

Watkins was aware, however, that if an artist lives up to these greater imaginative demands, his work will in the end acquire its audience. Having remained rigorously true to his principles, Watkins, for all his shunning of public acclaim, was quietly aware of the value of his work. He told his friend Dufau-Labeyrie, after listening to a radio broadcast: 'we heard MacNeice & Spender & Day Lewis & a few others. What a lot reputation does for people. My poems are better than theirs & nobody knows. Even you don't know. I say this from instinct, not pride.'[21]

He also said, in words which clearly apply to himself: 'The audience of a poet is always an audience in depth, and he mustn't really mind if even fifty years or a hundred go by before his work is felt by people exactly attuned to it, because that's happened to very great poets in the past.'[22] And again: 'I have remembered… that many great poets published little or nothing in their lifetimes, that publication and present audiences are an accident, however precious, and that poems that are genuine always eventually draw their audiences to them, unless they happen to be lost.'[23]

*

In 1935 Vernon Watkins, who was just beginning, after his new start, to discover his true poetic voice, met another young poet from the same town, who had just had his first book published – Dylan Thomas. An intense personal and working friendship developed between them. As Watkins describes: 'We became close friends almost immediately, from an affinity which I think we both recognised at once. That affinity was particularly clear when we talked about poetry or read it aloud.'[24] Thomas Taig, a theatre producer in Swansea, bears witness to this 'affinity':

> It was only when I… heard them repeating fragments of their latest poems that I began to understand the basis of their close friendship and their high esteem for each other both personally and professionally… there was never any talk… about aesthetic theories, philosophies or literary movements… the real interest lay in detailed discussion of the value of a particular syllable in a particular line and whether some word should be changed or deleted. There was no need to argue, for both moved freely in what I have called the inner world and both understood the arduous business of meticulous craftsmanship.[25]

What has, however, received as yet all too scant attention, is their completely opposite nature *as poets*. Vernon Watkins was an intensely musical poet, who wrote, as he put it: 'to an instrument'. This musical aspect is essential to Watkins's poetic gift: 'I believe that lyric poetry is closer to music than prose, and that it should be read exactly as a musical score.'[26] Michael Hamburger, praising the variety of Watkins's music, spoke of 'its extraordinary range of forms and metres, by no means always traditional, yet always mastered and made his own by an infallible ear'.[27]

His poetry only reveals itself when we respond to it musically. Kathleen Raine gives a telling description of the moment she first *heard* his poetry in this way, at a reading: 'For the first few minutes the ear was not attuned, as if to the speech of some celestial hierarchy not normally perceptible to human attention; but presently one heard and the voice of the poet became audible at once in the music and the meaning of the poetry.'[28]

In this he is radically different from Thomas, for if Watkins's poetry is predominantly *musical*, Thomas's is *sculptural*. Watkins was immediately aware of this difference when the two poets met: 'Our poetic methods were as unlike as possible, he beginning with a ball of phrases which he moulded into musical shape, and I with a musical cadence, almost out of earshot, to which I slowly gave substance. Although we had great affinity of theme our work was complementary.'[29] And again:

> We worked very differently. I must have written many hundreds of poems when I met him, working from the ear and for the ear. He worked from living language and from texture itself. *He moulded his poems. I heard mine.* Of course he listened too, with the greatest attention, wherever he put anything down, but he refused to let music take command in the early stages of composition.[30]

Dylan Thomas never described this complementarity with Watkins, but writing about his own preference in poetry, in 1935, he affirmed Watkins's characterisation of it: 'I think it should work from words, from the substance of words and the rhythm of substantial words set together, not towards words.'[31] Watkins gave a brief further glimpse into his own experience of hearing a 'musical cadence, almost out of earshot', in a letter about his long poem 'Yeats in Dublin': 'I have never heard a poem – not even

New Selected Poems

'Griefs of the Sea' which I *heard* coming out of the grass of the cliffs of Pennard and Hunt's Bay – in quite that way. What Yeats called an "articulation in the air". It was momentary and extraordinary. The whole poem took place in less than a second.'[32]

Their stylistic difference is, in the end, only part of a much wider complementary relationship between these two poet-friends, as fascinating in its interconnectedness as many another such literary friendship. Dylan Thomas, like Wordsworth, would often recapture in his writing the lost 'glory' of childhood; and, like Wordsworth, he even extended this vision back before birth. Wordsworth's 'trailing clouds of glory do we come' becomes, in Dylan Thomas's voice, 'Before I knocked and flesh let enter'.

Vernon Watkins's direction was opposite to this. Speaking of Thomas's 'beautiful poems evoking childhood', he remarked that Thomas 'could still go back to peace, but from there he could no longer go forward'.[33] His own very different model was Yeats: 'I... owed more to Yeats than to any other poet, as he had shown me something which the others had not been able to show; that is, how a lyric poet should grow old... I was astonished to find that his poetry increased in power until the moment of his death.'[34]

The threshold his own poetry addresses and crosses, repeatedly, is not that of birth but of death. Thus even of his first book he wrote: 'Every poem in the book rests upon the paradox of life being given back in imperishable terms after it had been logically surrendered to time and death. This is my particular country, my raison d'être, if you like.'[35]

This different relationship to youth and age is also reflected in the biography of their poetic output. In 1936, a year after their first meeting, Thomas, aged twenty-one, had already 'written about half the *Collected Poems* in their final or near-final versions, and drafted versions of another ten or so'.[36] In the last seven years of his life, by contrast, he completed only seven new poems. Vernon Watkins, at the same moment in 1936, aged twenty-eight, had early drafts, only, of no more than eight or nine poems included in his *Collected Poems*. The eighty-four poems in his first two posthumous collections, however, give evidence of the unceasing intensification of his poetry up until his death.

Perhaps the final difference between these two poets, the loud Dylan Thomas and the quiet Vernon Watkins, is in how their reputations developed after their deaths. Dylan Thomas acquired an almost iconic status. Vernon Watkins, by contrast, almost disappeared from popular sight. It might even be ventured that Dylan Thomas somehow became *too* famous and Vernon Watkins too unknown. The imbalance may gradually be redressed.

*

Vernon Watkins, when asked in a questionnaire 'For whom do you write?', replied: 'I am concerned chiefly with paradoxical truths', and my poems are addressed to those who underestimate the subtlety of life and death.'[37] In looking at the substance of Watkins's poetry, it is immediately clear that these 'paradoxical truths' are indeed at the core not only of everything he wrote, but also of his life: 'To believe in a paradox is a half-truth; the whole truth is to live it as well.'[38] I shall briefly explore this element of paradox in some of the most characteristic aspects of his work.

Watkins's poetry has sometimes been perceived as 'light' – as if it avoids the darker, more painful realities of life, for a too easily won transcendence. His own words give ample answer to this claim – for example, the very title of his poem 'Trust Darkness' or, from a letter, 'I have little use for a happiness which doesn't touch all the points of sorrow at the same time';[39] or, developing the paradox, 'Always it is from joy my music comes / And always it is sorrow keeps it true.'[40] In fact, Watkins's poetry contains a quite extraordinary strength, lightly worn. When he said of Dylan Thomas that after the Second World War 'he could still go back to peace, but from there he could no longer go forward', the same was clearly not true of Watkins himself. Watkins was obviously not a war poet, according to any customary definition. And yet, not only in poems written at the time but also in many others written afterwards, he addresses the spiritual situation faced by people at the time of the Second World War and in its aftermath. The poet David Wright made clear that Watkins was among those who had found a voice equal to this challenge: 'he is one of the very few who have the moral ability to scan the lineaments of our present predicament without turning into a stone, or rattling like a pebble. For the predicament in which we are all involved has now turned its face towards us, and that countenance is Gorgon: none can move and few can speak.'[41] Francis King, speaking of the poem 'The Broken Sea' in Watkins's second volume, published in 1945, noted the same qualities and strength: 'Mr Watkins has felt with peculiar intensity the horror of "the burning of an age"; but the poem does not lack hope. It is a hope which is only attained by passing through despair; it springs from knowledge of "the truth that abides in tears" – to use one of the poem's most haunting phrases. Nothing comparable has been published since *Little Gidding*.'[42]

Watkins himself, in a letter written during the war, pointed to his own awareness of the completely different demands on a poet during the Second as opposed to the First World War: 'You have a Wilfred Owen with you? Get one… and read "Exposure". I think I said in my paper it was the greatest war poem – I certainly told Eliot so. *But this war has something more, something inconceivable, only hinted at by Owen* in his Preface and "Strange Meeting".'[43]

This is an aspect of Watkins's work that has received almost no attention. Although he was in no sense a political poet, his ability to address the situation of his time, from his own perspective, is shown by a short piece about the Vietnam War, written in 1966:

I write as one totally unskilled in politics, yet deeply concerned with human behaviour. I am asked what I advocate as a solution. The first necessity is to end the fighting, the second to arrive at a just peace. The withdrawal of American troops, far from humiliating their country, would be an act of international heroism. There is no justification for war today, or… at any time in the future. Where evil exists it must be treated by peaceful means. The wounds of violence cannot be healed by violence. An enlightened nation is one that hates war.[44]

*

'Paradoxical truths' are equally the key to Watkins's relationship with the natural world. His appreciation of nature was not only remarkably fine and detailed, but also *tactile*: 'Touch a pine and the effect is quite extraordinary – the whole nature of the tree is changed. It leaps out of a photographic world into a breathing one. Then the scent of sweet-briar… We should touch, smell things always…'[45] After his death his friend Ceri Richards wrote about the Gower Peninsula, where they both lived: 'Now that he is not there any more the environment seems deprived and inarticulate.'[46] Watkins also said, however: 'I marvel at the beauty of landscape, *but I never think of it as a theme for poetry until I read metaphysical symbols behind what I see.'*[47]

Andrew Motion has complained that, with Watkins, 'specifics… are no sooner seen than they are mythologised or converted into abstracts to play their part in an inner theatre.'[48] For Watkins, however, the further level of meaning he seeks is neither added on to nature nor, as Motion suggests, abstracted from it. It *underlies* nature:

> For me, a poem that only reflects the natural world is an incomplete poem. I do not deny the bounty of nature, the inexhaustible secrets of the world that surrounds me, but something must be added by the poem itself. The addition depends on the poet's need. My own need, so far and I understand it, is the reality behind nature, the reality of which nature is a set of symbols, rather than nature itself.[49]

Kathleen Raine has well described how once we attend to Watkins's music, his intense perceptions of the natural world reveal themselves in their beauty and fineness of detail: 'Once attuned, the "minute particulars" come into focus; for in addressing the spirit no poet could be less abstract, less theoretical, less devotional, less "religious": we are shown the visible sensible world in all its precision of form, but in a different focus, so that at first we do not recognise in a transfigured landscape familiar headlands and hills.'[50]

*

Metaphysical or spiritual realities are, of course, at the core of Watkins's work. These may in themselves be off-putting for some people; yet we are not put off by the spirituality of Shelley or Blake or Yeats or Donne, or whoever else we might choose, as long as it heightens rather than hinders their art. When Watkins declares, 'For me, lyric poetry that is not exalted is not worth writing', he is in good company. But there has been a misapprehension that Watkins's spirituality is one-sided. A recent reviewer lamented: 'There is a difference between a poetry that looks to timelessness but also engages with the complexities of time and one that ignores time altogether.'[51] But paradox reigns, in Watkins's work, *even* with regard to spiritual realities. Nowhere is this clearer than in his relationship to the dead.

In many of his poems Watkins speaks of some kind of encounter or communion with the dead. The comparatively early poem 'Gravestones' ends: 'For the dead live / And I am of their kind.' 'Crowds' begins:

> Why should the living need my oil?
> I see them and their eyes are blest?
> No. For those others I must toil:
> I toil to set the dead at rest.

But 'Crowds' has *two* stanzas – the first about the dead, and the second about the living. 'If you would not disappoint the living, write for the dead,' wrote Watkins, but he knew that the reverse is also true: 'A good poem has two audiences: it is addressed to the living and the dead at the same time. If the poet dismisses the living he becomes morbid; if he dismisses the dead he ceases to be a prophet.'[52]

After Dylan Thomas's death, in 1953, this double truth became an urgent reality for Watkins. Death, we might say, became for him a matter of immediate life. This change points towards a feature of his Christological spirituality which has rarely been recognised. Despite his central, early experience of a reality beyond space and time, the direction of his spirituality and his poetry, as they evolved, was towards an ever-deepening relationship with the earth – with nature, with history and with other human beings.

Without some understanding of this change, a poem like 'Angel and Man' must seem a very strange one for Watkins to have written. The 'Angel' encourages 'Man' to a world of experience beyond this one, but 'Man' rejects this, if it denies his experience in this world. 'The Stayers' points in a similar direction. The poet Leslie Norris describes how Watkins increasingly 'treats... the natural world about him with the intensity he had reserved for the immortal world' and sees 'The Guest' as a masterly, late example of this.[53]

Failure to appreciate this has occasionally led to the view that Watkins's poems lack sufficient reference to events in this world. Because of Watkins's kinship with music, which must move us on its own terms, not on those of the occasions associated with it, he himself asks, in an aphorism: 'What is revision, except, in the interests of unity, to eliminate the evidence of words?' George Barker gave a striking contemporary response to this aspect of Watkins's poetry:

> His poems rise clear and straight out of the occasions and events that cause them; absolutely no alien matter accrues upon them, no dirt from the spade, no sediment from the placenta, no slivers from the rolled log, no prejudices from the personality, no indigestible portions that leopards reject: the poems are poems the way a Friday is a Friday.[54]

But Watkins knew well enough, regarding Dylan Thomas's poems, that 'just as "Over Sir John's Hill" can be better understood after seeing Laugharne, "Do Not Go Gentle Into That Good Night" can be better understood by knowing what Dylan's father was like.'[55] And the same is true of Watkins's own poems. There *are* specific references in his poems – and very often it greatly helps us to to be aware of these.

It is hard to imagine, for example, that 'The Exacting Ghost' would mean very much unless one knew that it was written after a deeply disturbing dream about Dylan Thomas, after the latter's death. The poem certainly comes into clear focus when one does. There are other poems – 'The Listening Days', for instance – where no such knowledge is necessary. Devotees may well choose to describe these in the same terms Watkins used about Yeats's work: 'lyric poetry… equal to any of the last 500 years – but of course time is of no account'.[56] But even these poems will remain inaudible unless we can relate their perceptions to our own.

Watkins's own task was clear, with regard to the *writing* of poetry: 'What matters is to get poems down. What matters is not to waste time on comment.'[57] But he was, of course, aware of the events his poems referred to – and often alluded to these at poetry readings, providing the audience with what small help they might need. 'The Feather', for example, will surely speak in any age. Something is added, however, by knowing it was written towards the end of the Second World War – and Watkins told his listeners so at readings.

Lack of clarity over this has led to perhaps the strangest criticism of all of Watkins – that, somehow, he didn't have a life, that he is a man with no biography. Thus Andrew Motion, after acknowledging that it might be helpful to know what gave rise to

Watkins's poems, declares that this cannot be done: 'One way of redeeming Watkins from neglect would be to socialise the work by showing how it related to the life... But in the sense that biographers use the phrase, Watkins didn't have much of a life.'[58]

A huge and detailed biography is in fact contained within Watkins's poems. 'The Muse of poetry is timeless,' wrote Watkins, adding: 'but a poet lives in time. His work is only complete if he observes two fidelities, one to his own experience and his own time, the other to the timeless and heroic truths with which he feels an imperceptible bond.'[59] He described his indebtedness to Yeats regarding the *personal* voice in lyric poetry: 'I was absorbed in Blake's Prophetic Books, but those tremendous visions... lacked personal statement, and this appeared in the new poems of Yeats with piercing clarity.'[60] All of Watkins's poems bear this personal relation, leaving within his work a sustained and intimate record of experience.

Watkins's dedication to the art of poetry might lead one to believe that, in Yeats's phrase, he had chosen 'perfection of the work' over that of the life. Philip Larkin, visiting Watkins after the war, in his cliff-top home in Gower, where he lived with his wife, Gwen, and five children, declared otherwise: 'his house... was smallish and chalet-like, but friendly and full of character – full, too, of books and children... It was no longer possible to think of his having rejected "perfection of the life" in exchange for literary mastery.'[61] Watkins himself also expressly stated: 'I am not saying that the need or ability to create art is the highest and most indispensable gift of man: *charity is clearly that.*'[62] The word 'charity', as in St Paul's 'faith, hope and charity', is rendered in contemporary translation as *love*.

The ultimate inseparability for Watkins of his art from his life, and from what he called 'the whole man's recurrent willingness to lose himself to an act of love',[63] was frequently born witness to by those who knew him. Larkin touched on this when he said that Watkins 'made it clear how one could, in fact, "live by poetry"'. Michael Hamburger, too, ended his memoir of Vernon Watkins: 'I cannot separate his work from his person... I shall never be able to read his poems without hearing his voice and seeing him as he was – one of the most admirable and lovable men it has been my good fortune to know.'[64]

*

There have to date been two clear phases in the reception of Watkins's work. The first was during his lifetime. His poetry was rarely, if ever, at the height of fashion, and, as we have seen, he had no intention of it becoming so. It was, however, constantly available from Faber; it was widely reviewed and held in high critical regard. He was undoubtedly not to everyone's poetic taste, but many could have affirmed Henry Reed's view: 'Vernon Watkins I have difficulty writing about. I find him at times very hard to understand, sometimes impossible; yet if a premature judgement may be allowed, I believe him to be the one poet of his generation who holds out unequivocal promise of greatness.'[65] As his poetry often addressed shared realities – everyone's experience, for example, of the Second World War – and as he was, after all, closely linked to the contemporary poetic community, his work was received in context. It belonged to the poetry of his time.

The second phase began after his death – particularly once Faber ceased publishing his work. His context was no longer shared and the manner of his poetry and his outlook on life were far from those that were popular; consequently, his poetry fell off the critical map. Those in the mainstream of poetic opinion gave his work little or no or negative attention.

There was also, however, during this second period, a hugely significant exception to this trend. Kathleen Raine, two years younger than Watkins, dedicated herself not only to her own poetry, but also to promoting the work of other poets and artists she recognised, often in the face of mainstream opinion. Raine consistently championed Watkins's work, writing introductions to two of his posthumous volumes of poetry and ensuring his work would often appear in *Temenos*, the journal she co-founded in 1981. In 1986 Golgonooza Press (run by Brian Keeble, a co-founder of *Temenos*) brought out, in a beautifully produced edition, *The Collected Poems of Vernon Watkins*. Readers did, therefore, continue to find their way to Watkins's work.

It is to be hoped that a third phase in the reception of his work may now come about. If *Temenos*'s approach to Watkins had a slight limitation, it perhaps focused too one-sidedly on the timeless aspect of his work, and was therefore not *paradoxical* enough. Thus the second period offered us either Watkins as a peripheral figure in the biographies of Dylan Thomas and Philip Larkin, or a timeless, soaring Watkins, freed of almost any earthly context. However, as Watkins has slowly disappeared from view, the need for a context against which to see him and his work has become ever greater. The extreme contrast between the responses of Kathleen Raine and Andrew Motion is, ultimately, an unnecessary one. Watkins must be reappraised as one of the major poets of his time, who had a unique voice and vision.

*

New Selected Poems contains poems from all the books Watkins prepared for publication, except for *The Lamp and the Veil*, whose three poems were considered too long to include. The epigram to 'The Childhood of Hölderlin' provides a single example of the many translations Watkins made – from German, French, Italian, Greek and Hungarian. The final section of the book contains several rarely published or unpublished poems, including one example of Watkins's light verse. The section concludes with some prose aphorisms, which give gnomic expression to many of Watkins's views on poetry. The notes, with some exceptions, are only to those poems Watkins himself commented on. There are also, within the notes, short comments on each of his books in sequence, in order to offer a very brief overview of his work.

Regarding the texts in *New Selected Poems*, although almost all of his poems went through an enormous number of drafts, Watkins was never in any doubt as to when a poem was in its final form. As he told his poetry students in America: 'Paper is cheap. Write hundreds of drafts. Your final draft should look as you had never revised at all.'[66] All the printed texts in the seven books he himself collected are therefore authoritative. These versions are exactly reproduced in *The Collected Poems of Vernon Watkins* and in the present volume.

With the collections prepared by others, after his death, the decisions over the chosen versions of poems were made in collaboration with Gwen Watkins, Kathleen Raine and Dr Ruth Pryor (*Uncollected Poems*), or with Gwen Watkins and Dr Ruth Pryor (*Ballad of the Outer Dark* and *The Breaking of the Wave*). Editorial comments in these three volumes, not reproduced here or in the *Collected Poems*, describe these textual choices. These versions were reprinted in *The Collected Poems of Vernon Watkins* and are reproduced here.

Regarding the section of 'Rarely Published and Unpublished Poems', four of the six poems are previously unpublished. The other two poems and the prose aphorisms were each published on a single occasion, in periodicals now out of print. References to these are included in the notes.

I am enormously grateful to Gwen Watkins, for her friendship and for her immediate support for this volume; to Archbishop Rowan Williams for so readily agreeing to write the foreword; and to Michael Schmidt and Judith Willson of Carcanet Press for their commitment to publishing it.

The last words on the book may happily be left to Vernon Watkins: 'If two people happen to see a good poem a considerable purpose may be served. The number of additional thousands is irrelevant. Again, a considerable purpose may be served if permanent poetry is made accessible, as it is in volume form, over a period of time, so that it may find its right audience.'

Notes

1 Henry Reed, 'Poetry in War Time; II – The Younger Poets', *The Listener*, 25 January 1945.
2 From 'Vernon Watkins and the Bardic Tradition' in Kathleen Raine, *Defending Ancient Springs*, Golgonooza Press, 1985.
3 From: *Aphorisms* (*X: A Quarterly*, 1960); *Poetry and Experience* (privately owned MS); Jenijoy La Belle, 'Vernon Watkins; Some Observations on Poetry', *The Anglo-Welsh Review*, No. 65, 1979.
4 'A Note on my Poetry' – National Library of Wales Manuscripts 22480E.
5 Notes for 'Cambridge Talk' – NLW MS 22480E.
6 'Poetry and the Audience' – NLW MS 22480E.
7 'A Note on my Poetry'– NLW MS 22480E.
8 'Address to Poetry Society, 1966', *Poetry Wales*, Vol. 12, No. 4, Spring 1977 (Vernon Watkins Special Number).
9 *Swansea and the Arts*, Ty Llên Publications, 2000.
10 'Sonnet of Resurrection 7'.
11 'Poetry and the Audience'.
12 'A Note on my Poetry'.
13 'Poetry and the Audience'.
14 'A Note on my Poetry'.
15 Notes for 'Cambridge Talk'.
16 Gwen Watkins, *Dylan Thomas: Portrait of a Friend*, Y Lolfa, Talybont, 2005.
17 *Poetry and a Career* – privately owned MS.
18 Letter to Peter Hellings, 2 July 1939, privately owned.

19 Notebook entry, 1966; quoted in Gwen Watkins, 'A Poet in Miniature', *New Welsh Review*, No. 50, 2000.
20 'Problems of Communication', *The Listener*, 71, 1964.
21 Letter to Francis Dufau-Labeyrie; autumn 1938. Privately owned.
22 *The Poet Speaks. Interviews with contemporary poets*, Routledge, 1966.
23 Reply to a questionnaire, 1959; privately owned.
24 *Dylan Thomas: Letters to Vernon Watkins*, Dent/Faber, London, 1957.
25 Thomas Taig, 'Swansea between the Wars', in *The Anglo-Welsh Review*, Vol. 17, No. 39, Summer 1968.
26 'Context', *The London Magazine*, February 1962.
27 Michael Hamburger, 'Vernon Watkins, a Memoir', in *Vernon Watkins 1906–1967*, ed. Leslie Norris, Faber, London, 1970.
28 Kathleen Raine, 'The Poetry of Vernon Watkins', in *Vernon Watkins 1906–1967*.
29 'For Whom does a Poet Write?', *Temenos 1*, London, 1981.
30 'Reading of Poems to the Staff Club, Swansea University', 22 February 1967; privately owned MS. (Emphasis added.)
31 Letter to Charlie Fisher, 1935, in *Dylan Thomas. The Collected Letters*, ed. Paul Ferris, Dent, London, 2000.
32 Letter to F. Dufau-Labeyrie, in *Temenos 8*, London, 1987.
33 Afterword to *Adventures in the Skin Trade*, Signet Classics, New York, 1961.
34 From 'Lectures on Modern Poetry', in *Poetry Wales*, Vol. 12, No. 4, 1977; and 'Poets and the Reading of Poetry' – NLW MS 22480E.
35 *Poetry and Experience*; privately owned MS.
36 Paul Ferris, *Dylan Thomas. The Biography*, Phoenix, London, 2000.
37 Questionnaire in *Wales, 23*, 1946.
38 *Articulations*, May 1955. In *Poetry Wales*, Spring 1977, Vol. 12, No. 4.
39 Letter to Dufau-Labeyrie, in *Temenos 8*.
40 'Sonnet: to Certain Ancient Anonymous Poets'. (Not included in the present selection.)
41 'Essay on Vernon Watkins', David Wright, *Nimbus,* Vol. 3, No. 1, Spring 1955.
42 Francis King, review of *The Lamp and the Veil*, *The Listener*, 6 December 1945.
43 Letter to Peter Hellings, 13 January 1944. (Emphasis added.)
44 From *Authors take sides on the Vietnam War*, ed. Cecil Woolf and John Bagguley, Peter Owen, London, 1967.
45 Letter to F. Dufau-Labeyrie, in *Temenos 8*.
46 'Remembering Vernon', Ceri Richards, in *Vernon Watkins 1906–1967*.
47 *Poetry and Experience*. (Emphasis added.)
48 Andrew Motion, 'Going into the Dark', review of *Collected Poems of Vernon Watkins*, *TLS*, 3 July 1987.
49 'Introduction to a Reading at Carmarthen', 8 February 1967; NLW MS 22480E.
50 See note 28.
51 William Wootten, 'In the Graveyard of Verse', review of *Collected Poems of Vernon Watkins*, *London Review of Books*, 9 August 2000.
52 Broadcast Script, 1947; NLW MS 22480E.
53 Leslie Norris, 'Seeing Eternity: Vernon Watkins and the Poet's Task', in *Triskel Two*, Christopher Davies, Llandybie, 1973.
54 George Barker, Review of 'The Lady with the Unicorn', *Life and Letters*, Vol. LX, No. 138, February 1949.
55 'Eight Poems by Dylan Thomas', 1955; privately owned MS.

Introduction

56 Letter to F. Dufau-Labeyrie, in *Temenos 8*.

57 Notebook entry, quoted in Gwen Watkins, 'A Poet in Miniature', *New Welsh Review*, No. 50, Autumn 2000.

58 See note 48.

59 *Poetry and Experience.*

60 *Poetry and Experience.*

61 Philip Larkin, 'Vernon Watkins: An Encounter and a Re-encounter', quoted in *Vernon Watkins 1906–1967*.

62 'The Need of the Artist', *The Listener*, 8 November 1962. (Emphasis added.)

63 Prose note to 'The Death Bell' in *The Collected Poems of Vernon Watkins*.

64 Michael Hamburger, *Vernon Watkins, a Memoir*, quoted in *Vernon Watkins 1906–1967*.

65 See note 1.

66 Jenijoy La Belle, 'Vernon Watkins; Some Observations on Poetry', in *Anglo-Welsh Review*, No. 65, 1979.

The Collier

When I was born on Amman hill
A dark bird crossed the sun.
Sharp on the floor the shadow fell;
I was the youngest son.

And when I went to the County School
I worked in a shaft of light.
In the wood of the desk I cut my name:
Dai for Dynamite.

The tall black hills my brothers stood;
Their lessons all were done.
From the door of the school when I ran out
They frowned to watch me run.

The slow grey bells they rung a chime
Surly with grief or age.
Clever or clumsy, lad or lout,
All would look for a wage.

I learnt the valley flowers' names
And the rough bark knew my knees.
I brought home trout from the river
And spotted eggs from the trees.

A coloured coat I was given to wear
Where the lights of the rough land shone.
Still jealous of my favour
The tall black hills looked on.

They dipped my coat in the blood of a kid
And they cast me down a pit,
And although I crossed with strangers
There was no way up from it.

Soon as I went from the County School
I worked in a shaft. Said Jim,
'You will get your chain of gold, my lad,
But not for a likely time.'

And one said, 'Jack was not raised up
When the wind blew out the light
Though he interpreted their dreams
And guessed their fears by night.'

And Tom, he shivered his leper's lamp
For the stain that round him grew;
And I heard mouths pray in the after-damp
When the picks would not break through.

They changed words there in darkness
And still through my head they run,
And white on my limbs is the linen sheet
And gold on my neck the sun.

Griefs of the Sea

It is fitting to mourn dead sailors,
To crown the sea with some wild wreath of foam
On some steep promontory, some cornercliff of Wales
Though the deaf wave hear nothing.

It is fitting to fling off clothing,
To enter the sea with plunge of seawreaths white
Broken by limbs that love the waters, fear the stars,
Though the blind wave grope under eyes that see, limbs that
wonder,
Though the blind wave grope forward to the sand
With a greedy, silvered hand.

It is a horrible sound, the low wind's whistle
Across the seaweeds on the beach at night.
From stone to stone through hissing caves it passes
Up the curved cliff and shakes the prickly thistle
And spreads its hatred through the grasses.

In spite of that wicked sound
Of the wind that follows us like a scenting hound,
It is fitting on the curved cliff to remember the drowned,
To imagine them clearly for whom the sea no longer cares,
To deny the language of the thistle, to meet their foot-firm tread
Across the dark-sown tares
Who were skilful and erect, magnificent types of godhead,
To resist the dogging wind, to accuse the sea-god;
Yet in that gesture of anger we must admit
We were quarrelling with a phantom unawares.

For the sea turns whose every drop is counted
And the sand turns whose every grain a holy hour-glass holds
And the weeds turn beneath the sea, the sifted life slips free,
And the wave turns surrendering from its folds
All things that are not sea, and thrown off is the spirit
By the sea, the riderless horse which they once mounted.

from *The Ballad of the Mari Lwyd* (1941)

Two Decisions

I must go back to Winter,
The dark, confiding tree,
The sunflower's eaten centre
That waved so tenderly;
Go back, break fellowship
With bud and leaf,
Break the loud branch and strip
The stillborn grief.
I must restore the thorn,
The naked sentinel,
Call lash of hail, wind-scorn
To laughter's lintel;
End argument in a way
Sudden and swift,
Leave stillness, go away
Beyond this leaf-drift,
Leave the ten-windowed house
And merely remark,
The ivy grew too close:
That house was dark.

Then I look out:
Rut, road and hill I see.
Tracks turn about.
Winter must come to me.
I shall not go,
I shall wait here
Until the snow
Bury the old year,
Until the swallows are gone
And the lintels wet
Tell that the rain that has blown
Is blowing yet.
Let me be nowhere
A melodramatic guest
Since here as anywhere
The light is best.

Though distant things entreat
The afraid, the fanciful,
The near is faithful:
Do not deny it.

Stone Footing

Stopping my ears to Venus and her doves,
I steal stone footing, find death's carved decree;
I choose this path, the rock which no man loves
Familiar to birds, cast by a barren sea.
Cold on this ridge among the breeding winds,
Starved in the famine forced by Adam's rib,
Here I hold breath, knowing the door of my friends
Is rock, and I am exiled from their tribe.
I put my ear to the ground, I plant my foot
Against grey rock, but wind and seawave smother
The stone's coiled fossil-saga; this navel-knot
Fastens my moving to the great rock-mother.
I would unchain them; but there flies that other
Bearing the sea, and kills me with her shot.

from *Ballad of the Mari Lwyd*

Midnight. Midnight. Midnight. Midnight.
Hark at the hands of the clock.
Now dead men rise in the frost of the stars
And fists on the coffins knock.
They dropped in their graves without one sound;
Then they were steady and stiff.
But now they tear through the frost of the ground
As heretic, drunkard and thief.

Why should you fear though they might pass
Ripping the stitch of grief,
The white sheet under the frosted glass,
Crisp and still as a leaf?
Or look through sockets that once were eyes
At the table and white cloth spread?
The terrible, picklock Charities
Raised the erected dead.

Under your walls they gnaw like mice;
Virtue is unmasked.
The hands of the clock betray your vice.
They give what none has asked.
For they have burrowed beneath the graves
And found what the good gave most:
Refuse cast by the righteous waves
In fossil, wraith and ghost.

Chalice and Wafer. Wine and Bread.
And the picklock, picklock, picklock tread.

Midnight. Midnight. Midnight. Midnight.
Hark at the hands of the clock.

*

Out in the night the nightmares ride;
And the nightmares' hooves draw near.
Dead men pummel the panes outside,
And the living quake with fear.
Quietness stretches the pendulum's chain
To the limit where terrors start,
Where the dead and the living find again
They beat with the selfsame heart.

In the coffin-glass and the window-pane
You beat with the selfsame heart.

Midnight. Midnight. Midnight. Midnight.
Hark at the hands of the clock.

(Very faint)
'We bring from white Hebron
And Ezekiel's Valley,
From the dead sea of Harlech
And mountain-girt Dolgelley,
All that singing way
From Cader to Kidwelly,
A stiff, a star-struck thing
Blown by the stinging spray
And the stinging light of the stars,
Our white, stiff thing,
Death and breath of the frost,
That has known the room of glass,
Dropped by the Milky Way
To the needle and thread of the pass.'

*

'In the black of the churchyard yew we lay
And the long roots taught us much.
We groped for the sober light of day,
Light that we dared not touch.
The sleet of the stars fell cold and thin
Till we turned, and it touched our crown;
Then we yearned for the heat in the marrow of sin,
For the fire of a drinkers' town.'

Sinner and saint, sinner and saint:
A horse's head in the frost.

'But brightest brimstone light on him
And burn his rafters black
That will not give when his fears are dim
The treasure found in the sack.
In the mouth of the sack, in the stifled breath,
In the sweat of the hands, in the noose,
In the black of the sack, in the night of death
Shines what you dare not lose.'

Midnight. Midnight. Midnight. Midnight.
Hark at the hands of the clock.

from *The Ballad of the Mari Lwyd* (1941)   7

'Under the womb of teeming night
Our Mari tries your faith;
And She has Charity's crown of light:
Spectre she knows and wraith;
How sweet-tongued children are wickedly born
By a swivelling devil's thrust
Mounting the night with a murderous horn,
Riding the starry gust.'

*

Go back, with your drowned and drunken eyes
And your crooked mouths so small
And your Mari foaled of the starry skies:
Go back to the seawave's fall.
If we lift and slide the bolt in the door
What can our warm beer buy?
What can you give for the food we store
But a slice of starving sky?

Sinner and saint, sinner and saint:
A horse's head in the frost.

Midnight. Midnight. Midnight. Midnight.
Hark at the hands of the clock.

'O who has woven the skein of the hair,
And who has knotted the ropes of the fist,
And who has hollowed the bones of the eyes?
One of you answer: the hands have kissed.
I see in your eyes white terror,
I see in your locked hands hate.
Press, we are one step nearer
The live coals in the grate.'

Midnight. Midnight. Midnight. Midnight.
Hark at the hands of the clock.

The slinking dead, the shrinking sands,
And the picklock, picklock, picklock hands.

New Selected Poems

Hark, they are going; the footsteps shrink,
And the sea renews her cry.
The big stars stare and the small stars wink;
The Plough goes glittering by.
It was a trick of the turning tide
That brought those voices near.
Dead men pummelled the panes outside:
We caught the breath of the year.

(Voice)
Dread and quiet, evil and good:
Frost in the night has mixed their blood.

Thieving and giving, good and evil:
The beggar's a saint, and the saint a devil.

Mari Lwyd, Lwyd Mari:
A sacred thing through the night they carry.

Betrayed are the living, betrayed the dead:
All are confused by a horse's head.

Midnight. Midnight. Midnight. Midnight.
Hark at the hands of the clock.
Lazarus comes in a shroud so white
Out of the hands of the clock.
While baskets are gathered of loaves of light,
Rape is picking the lock.
Hungering fingers, bones of the night,
Knock, knock, knock.

from
The Lady with the Unicorn
(1948)

Music of Colours: White Blossom

White blossom, white, white shell; the Nazarene
Walking in the ear; white touched by souls
Who know the music by which white is seen,
Blinding white, from strings and aureoles,
Until that is not white, seen at the two poles,
Nor white the Scythian hills, nor Marlowe's queen.

The spray looked white until this snowfall.
Now the foam is grey, the wave is dull.
Call nothing white again, we were deceived.
The flood of Noah dies, the rainbow is lived.
Yet from the deluge of illusions an unknown colour is saved.

White must die black, to be born white again
From the womb of sounds, the inscrutable grain,
From the crushed, dark fibre, breaking in pain.

The bud of the apple is already forming there.
The cherry-bud, too, is firm, and behind it the pear
Conspires with the racing cloud. I shall not look.
The rainbow is diving through the wide-open book
Past the rustling paper of birch, the sorceries of bark.

Buds in April, on the waiting branch,
Starrily opening, light raindrops drench,
Swinging from world to world when starlings sweep,
Where they alight in air, are white asleep.
They will not break, not break, until you say
White is not white again, nor may may.

White flowers die soonest, die into that chaste
Bride-bed of the moon, their lives laid waste.
Lilies of Solomon, taken by the gust,
Sigh, make way. And the dark forest
Haunts the lowly crib near Solomon's dust,
Rocked to the end of majesty, warmed by the low beast,
Locked in the liberty of his tremendous rest.

If there is white, or has been white, it must have been
When His eyes looked down and made the leper clean.
White will not be, apart, though the trees try
Spirals of blossom, their green conspiracy.
She who touched His garment saw no white tree.

Lovers speak of Venus, and the white doves,
Jubilant, the white girl, myth's whiteness, Jove's,
Of Leda, the swan, whitest of his loves.
Lust imagines him, web-footed Jupiter, great down
Of thundering light; love's yearning pulls him down
On the white swan-breast, the magical lawn,
Involved in plumage, mastered by the veins of dawn.

In the churchyard the yew is neither green nor black.
I know nothing of Earth or colour until I know I lack
Original white, by which the ravishing bird looks wan.
The mound of dust is nearer, white of mute dust that dies
In the soundfall's great light, the music in the eyes,
Transfiguring whiteness into shadows gone,
Utterly secret. I know you, black swan.

from *The Lady with the Unicorn* (1948)   11

The Feather

I stoop to gather a seabird's feather
Fallen on the beach,
Torn from a beautiful drifting wing;
What can I learn or teach,
Running my finger through the comb
And along the horny quill?
The body it was torn from
Gave out a cry so shrill,
Sailors looked from their white road
To see what help was there.
It dragged the winds to a drop of blood
Falling through drowned air,
Dropping from the sea-hawk's beak,
From frenzied talons sharp;
Now if the words they lost I speak
It must be to that harp
Under the strange, light-headed sea
That bears a straw of the nest.
Unless I make that melody,
How can the dead have rest?

Sheer from wide air to the wilderness
The victim fell, and lay;
The starlike bone is fathomless,
Lost among wind and spray.
This lonely, isolated thing
Trembles amid their sound.
I set my finger on the string
That spins the ages round.
But let it sleep, let it sleep
Where shell and stone are cast;
Its ecstasy the Furies keep,
For nothing here is past.
The perfect into night must fly;
On this the winds agree.
How could a blind rock satisfy
The hungers of the sea?

Crowds

Why should the living need my oil?
I see them, and their eyes are blest.
No. For those others I must toil:
I toil to set the dead at rest.

Yet when I watch in solemn tides
The drifting crowds, each life a ghost,
I mourn them, for their truth abides;
Nor is one loved, till he is lost.

Lover and Girl

You have opened the graves
And unbarred the door of the sea.
You have turned the barren waves
To blossoms upon life's tree.
Why seems it the ocean no longer accuses and raves?

'You were changed by me.'

You were patient as flame
Lit for the souls of the dead.
The barren women came,
Knocked, and were comforted.
What word was it passed when you gave me that power to reclaim?

'Nothing I said.'

When we stood by the sheaves,
I looked, and, no longer estranged,
Saw the chestnut ripening in leaves
Wild breath disarranged.
Who drew my eyes forth to the loom till they saw how it weaves?

from *The Lady with the Unicorn* (1948)   13

'I said you were changed.'

Yet the mystery goes
Still deeper, that brought it to pass.
In the grave you transfigured the rose,
Springing changed in the grass.
Where found you this lightning that alters the bloom where it
grows?

In what burning-glass?

Gravestones

Look down. The dead have life.
Their dreadful night accompanies our Springs.
Touch the next leaf:
Such darkness lives there, where a last grief sings.

Light blinds the whirling graves.
Lost under rainwet earth the letters run.
A finger grieves,
Touching worn names, bearing daughter and son.

Here the quick life was borne,
A fountain quenched, fountains with sufferings crowned.
Creeds of the bone
Summoned from darkness what no Sibyl found.

Truly the meek are blest
Past proud men's trumpets, for they stilled their fame
Till this late blast
Gave them their muted, and their truest name.

Sunk are the stones, green-dewed,
Blunted with age, touched by cool, listening grass.
Vainly these died,
Did not miraculous silence come to pass.

14   New Selected Poems

Yet they have lovers' ends,
Lose to hold fast, as violets root in frost.
With stronger hands
I see them rise through all that they have lost.

I take a sunflower down,
With light's first faith persuaded and entwined.
Break, buried dawn,
For the dead live, and I am of their kind.

The Listening Days

Morning of light, I wake.
The waves and watersprings,
Birdsong and leaves that shake,
Proclaim created things.
The laughing wind lifts branches through the air;
All that I touched is truthful, and is fair.

Now, in the height of noon,
No shadow here is seen;
But shades will lengthen soon,
Stretching across the green.
He pours down thought and fills me with lost light;
Yet who loved day, that loves not starry night?

The words we speak are low:
They linger near the path.
We are upheld, I know,
By those who died in faith.
They are about us now who can fulfil
All when the wind has dropped, and when the boughs are still.

from *The Lady with the Unicorn* (1948)   15

Time's Deathbed

I went to bed with time.
Through the blue dark, sublime,
I watched Orion rise
And all the stars' fireflies
Through distance climb.

Quite still I lay awake,
Hearing time's spectre make
Dynastic moan, more far
Than midnight's millionth star,
For love's dead sake.

Softly the curtain flapped
As though a ball had dapped
And then bounced out again;
And through my brain
Thoughts travelled and were trapped.

The universe enshrined
Stared from my mummied mind;
I heard my beating blood:
One near me stood.
I smiled inside the wind.

I listened. Time like sand
Slid through a hidden hand;
Although no step was heard,
It seemed a shadow stirred:
My dark was manned.

Then, while I listened still,
A voice from near the sill
More low, more wavering
Than curlew's call in Spring,
Made my flesh thrill:

'Possess new time, possess
New time, or nothingness.
The spoils of sleep
That other gives. I keep
Spoil-spurning nakedness.'

Desire contended there
With one so fair,
My pulse stopped as I turned
To that new life which burned
With upright hair.

Then sprang a sweat of fear,
For where soul thrust a spear
Blood rose immense,
The light was so intense,
The shade so near.

Then, when all thoughts were summed
And the small flies had hummed
Around the passive bone,
I gave so great a groan
That time was dumbed.

Deeper and far more tender
That groan to my life-lender
Floated, than songs of praise,
For the firm pulse of days
Was locked in my surrender.

Once more the Near One spoke:
'Lie still. Your fist then broke
The hour-glass that has cursed
Man from the first
With superstition's cloak.

from *The Death Bell* (1954)   17

Time built your room three-walled
Where Fear, a nursling, crawled,
But at the fourth wall I
Bring the starred sky
And the scented world.'

Confusion of the dark,
Snuffing of the spark,
Unclothed the shades
For which we had used spades
In the priests' sad park.

Confusion tenebrous
Brought spoilers covetous,
But naked in the sheet
It was uniquely sweet
To lie so generous.

The Dead Shag

Shag: a mummified bird.
The sea-flash never is still.
I have watched long, long,
The craning neck that stirred
To the fisherman's lightest sound.
Jet-winged skimmer of sea
Sped from the leaning hill;
Under my net I found
A blackened piece of a tree,
Touched through the brilliant curd
Of spray, a cold black thing;
Then at once I caught the thrill
Of a wing in the fire-wake charred.
Shag: a mummified bird.
The sea-flash never is still.

I did not expect that knot
Of black in the hollow pool.
I have watched long, long,
This glancing fisher-bird, shot
With every silk of the rock,
Rising in foam, then sheer
Dive through the spindrift spool
Under the herring-gulls' flock,
Always to reappear
In an unpredictable spot.
The light in the eye had set;
As I touched the rigid flesh,
Under my net it stayed
Sunken, the eye of jade
Seen through a narrow mesh.

Taut, hard to forget,
This under-water bird
Glistening, glistening low,
Would vanish under the net
Of waves, where vision would rest
On beams, till at last a speck
Emerged, a questioning head
Buoyed up between crest and crest.
I have watched the straining neck
Streaming on wind to set
Its wonder back in a wedge,
Then, its orbit ended, stop
On a ledge that overhung
Plumb chaos, where seabirds swung
But only their shades would drop.

Near to that meeting-place,
A guano-whitened rock,
Listening, listening low,
Hidden flat on my face
In grass, I have heard the wail
Of bird by eel-dark bird
Surveying the pitch and knock
Of the breakers' punishing flail,
Where the lightest trespassing word
Would prompt an exodus race,
A movement start like a shot
Each anchorite from its mark
To safety out in the bay.
I have lost the light of day
If once I have lost that dark.

The Shell

Who could devise
But the dark sea this thing
Of depth, of dyes
Claws of weed cling,
Whose colour cries:
'I am of water, as of air the wing',
Yet holds the eyes
As though they looked on music perishing?

Yet the shell knows
Only its own dark chamber
Coiled in repose
Where without number
One by one goes
Each blind wave, feeling mother-of-pearl and amber,
Flooding, to close
A book all men might clasp, yet none remember.

Too far away
For thought to find the track,
Sparkling with spray
Rose, green and black,
The colours play,
Strained by the ebb, revealing in the wrack
The myth of day,
A girl too still to call her bridegroom back.

There falls the weight
Of glory unpossessed;
There the sands late
Hold the new guest
Whose ponderous freight
Draws the pool's hollow like a footprint pressed.
Its outcast state
Suddenly seems miraculous and blest.

Turn it; now hold
Its ancient heart. How fair
With lost tales told
In sea-salt air
Light's leaf-of-gold
Leaps from the threshold up the spiral stair,
Then lost, is cold,
Bound in a flash to rock with Ariadne's hair.

from *The Death Bell* (1954)

Art and the Ravens

Art holds in wind the way the ravens build
Breeding, flying, and still the thread holds fast.
Birth cries out, flying; and where the cry is stilled
Substance gives way, the talon grips the Past.
At the rock's foot fossils and wrecks are cast.
Still the cry wanders, though the cry is stilled.
Art holds in wind the way the ravens build.

Stand to time now, my Muse,
Unwavering, like this rock
The mated ravens use,
Building against the shock
Of dawn, a throne in air
Above the labouring sea,
Yet fine as a child's hair
Because great industry
Accomplishes no art
To match the widespread wing
Riding the heavens apart.
A lost, yet living thing.

Stumbling their rock-rung way,
I startle them. They drop
Over the verge of day,
Buoyed by the sea-wind up.
Then, seeing my shade molest
The gaunt and threadbare place
Where hangs their windy nest,
See with what towering grace,
As wave's ninth wonder whirls
Its fleece against that wall,
He superb wings unfurls
With talons poised, to fall.

O great, O guardian strength
Vertical power of wings,
True plummet found at length
By devious reckonings,
Your skirmishings protect
Love's brood, the hidden young,
By piercing intellect
High in the balance hung.
Far down, the breakers prove
Accomplishment all vain
Till art, the body of love,
Is won from death again.

One raven floats away
To scour the wrack and glide
Raucous above the bay,
Returning soon in pride
To perch upon this crest
Whose hollows fill the air
With voice on voice at rest
Lost in the breakers there.
And then both ravens give
Their dark fair-weather cry,
Watching the wild earth live
From those twin points of sky.

O dark, interior flame,
O spring Elijah struck:
Obscurity is fame;
Glory and praise are luck.
Nothing can live so wild
As those ambitious wings
Majestic, for love's child
Defending ancient springs.
Drifting in light, they stall.
Winds' conflict keeps them true.
Sunbeam and breaker's fall
Confound them. They cut through.

from *The Death Bell* (1954)

Art holds in wind the way the ravens build
Breeding, flying, and still the thread holds fast.
Crag falls to crag; and where that cry is stilled,
Under black wings the talon grips the Past.
At the rock's foot fossils and wrecks are cast.
The sky is falling: distance is fulfilled.
Art holds in wind the way the ravens build.

Taliesin in Gower

Late I return, O violent, colossal, reverberant, eavesdropping sea.
My country is here. I am foal and violet. Hawthorn breaks from
                                                    my hands.
I watch the inquisitive cormorant pry from the praying rock of
                                                    Pwlldu,
Then skim to the gulls' white colony, to Oxwich's cockle-strewn
                                                    sands.

I have seen the curlew's triangular print, I know every inch of his
                                                    way.
I have gone through the door of the foundered ship, I have slept
                                                    in the winch of the cave
With pine-log and unicorn-spiral shell secreting the colours of day;
I have been taught the script of the stones, and I know the tongue
                                                    of the wave.

I witness here in a vision the landscape to which I was born,
Three smouldering bushes of willow, like trees of fire, and the
                                                    course
Of the river under the stones of death, carrying the ear of corn
Withdrawn from the moon-dead chaos of rocks overlooking its
                                                    secret force.

I see, a marvel in Winter's marshes, the iris break from its sheath
And the dripping branch in the ache of sunrise frost and shadow
redeem
With wonder of patient, living leaf, while Winter, season of death,
Rebukes the sun, and grinds out men's groans in the voice of its
underground stream.

Yet now my task is to weigh the rocks on the level wings of a bird,
To relate these undulations of time to a kestrel's motionless poise.
I speak, and the soft-running hour-glass answers; the core of the
rock is a third:
Landscape survives, and these holy creatures proclaim their
regenerate joys.

I know this mighty theatre, my footsole knows it for mine.
I am nearer the rising pewit's call than the shiver of her own wing.
I ascend in the loud waves' thunder, I am under the last of the nine.
In a hundred dramatic shapes I perish, in the last I live and sing.

All that I see with my sea-changed eyes is a vision too great for
the brain.
The luminous country of auk and eagle rocks and shivers to earth.
In the hunter's quarry this landscape died; my vision restores it
again.
These stones are prayers; every boulder is hung on a breath's
miraculous birth.

Gorse breaks on the steep cliff-side, clings earth, in patches
blackened for sheep,
For grazing fired; now the fair weather comes to the ravens'
pinnacled knoll.
Larks break heaven from the thyme-breathing turf; far under,
flying through sleep,
Their black fins cutting the rainbow surf, the porpoises follow
the shoal.

from *The Death Bell* (1954)   25

They are gone where the river runs out, there where the breakers
divide
The lacework of Three Cliffs Bay in a music of two seas;
A heron flaps where the sandbank holds a dyke to the twofold tide,
A wave-encircled isthmus of sound which the white
bird-parliament flees.

Rhinoceros, bear and reindeer haunt the crawling glaciers of age
Beheld in the eye of the rock, where a javelin'd arm held stiff,
Withdrawn from the vision of flying colours, reveals, like script
on a page,
The unpassing moment's arrested glory, a life locked fast in the
cliff.

Now let the great rock turn. I am safe with an ear of corn,
A repository of light once plucked, from all men hidden away.
I have passed through a million changes. In a butterfly coracle
borne,
My faith surmounting the Titan, I greet the prodigious bay.

I celebrate you, marvellous forms. But first I must cut the wood,
Exactly measure the strings, to make manifest what shall be.
All Earth being weighed by an ear of corn, all heaven by a drop
of blood.
How shall I loosen this music to the listening, eavesdropping sea?

Ballad of the Rough Sea

I like the smell of the wind, the sniff,
Said a man on the top of Dover cliff.
I like the voice of the sea, the sound,
Said the fossil-man asleep in the ground.
And I want to look over the sea,
Said the man on the cliff-top free.
I want to look over the sea,
I will look over the sea.

The sun fell slant on the cliff's white face
And the waters ran under the sails in a race
But the fossil-man in his bed of chalk
Turned in his grave and began to talk:
O what's the good of a man in a rock
Who will not wake when the seawaves knock?
I want to stand up in the rock,
I will stand up in the rock.

O the seagulls are crying, the seagulls scream
That the sea is cruel and blue and green
But to-day the waters are white with spray
And hark in the boats what the fishermen say:
'It's a rough grey day with the tide coming in
And a haul of herring's a slippery skin
For the waters are deep and the nets are thin.
It's a rough grey day with the tide coming in.'

The fishers were fishing in little boats
From Cap Grisnez to John o' Groats
When the man in the rock and the man on the cliff
Met, like a shadow sheer and stiff.
They were shooting their hooks from the side
And the wind coming in with the tide.
They were leaning and looking over the side.
They were shooting their hooks from the side.

from *The Death Bell* (1954)

There's a phantom above the seawaves' roar
Screams, and a man has come through the door
Of the chalkwhite cliff, and star and sea
Are locked in the fear of a fisherman's knee,
But louder and louder the white waves hiss –
They will never come out of this.
Till the stars fall and the stone mouths kiss
They will never come out of this.

Come up from the sea, you sandy shoals
That lurk where Leviathan swims and rolls!
Like the pointed limpets stung by foam
Bared by the black wave leaping home
Come up from the sea, you crags,
Where the soaked straw-pillow sags,
Come up for the wreck's black-timbered rags,
Come up from the sea, you crags.

'O wandering water white and free
As the runaway stag that hides in the tree,
As the runaway stag that flies from the horn,
Fly to the low roof where we were born
And pull the door from the hinge and throw
The seven wild windows all in a row
And the tables and chairs in the room below
Through the white sea-jaws throw!

There are loaves of bread in the wooden chest
And safe on the hooks the white cups rest
And high on the shelf are sugar and tea
But cold is the darkness under the sea.
There's a floor unsafe beneath
And the sea has a wolf's white teeth.
O sweet would it be to beg and breathe.
There's a floor unsafe beneath.

O gallows-man on the cliff-top free,
Why do you fix your eyes on the sea?
O man in the rock erect and stiff,
Why are you pale as the dead white cliff?
O is it your thought and is it your wish
To help us to catch a creel of fish?
The waters to-night are devilish.
O tell us your thought and your wish.'

I have left in a room my rope and pin.
I will open your eyes when the sea rolls in.
I have left in a cave my bony skull.
I am waiting to hear the cry of a gull
For a seagull is crying aloud
That the sea is white as a shroud,
That, whiter than whitest moon or cloud,
The sea is white as a shroud.

'Go back to your rock, go back to your room.
We are men of heart, not men of the tomb.
Not the sea's twist nor the wind's alarms
Shall pull us down from the New Moon's arms,
And our ships are good black teak.
Go back, for we must not speak.
Go back to the crevice, back to the creek.
Go back, for we must not speak.'

from *The Death Bell* (1954)

from
Cypress and Acacia
(1959)

Three Harps

Ambitions playing:
The first, inseparable
From gold-edged printing
On Daedalus' table.

Desire for flight;
Chariot-usurping skill.
The god of light
Torn from the godlike will.

What tears of amber,
What pre-natal force
From dawn's dark chamber
Fired me on my course?

Three harps: one
From emulation drew its strength.
The rising sun:
A harp at arm's length.

The second word of day;
The second word:
A harp a hand away
Held by a human cord.

By cypress taught and yew,
My soul I made
Write old ambition new
And qualify the laurel's shade.

I set one grave apart,
Gave speech to stone:
'Come back to my sad heart
And play this harp of bone.'

Little for the sun I cared,
Little for renown.
I saw the unknown, unshared,
True grave. So I lay down;

Lay down, and closed my eyes
To the end of all time,
The end of birth's enterprise
And death's small crime.

Then at once the shrouded harp
Was manifest. I began
To touch, though pain is sharp,
The ribs of the man.

Taliesin and the Spring of Vision

'I tread the sand at the sea's edge, sand of the hour-glass,
And the sand receives my footprint, singing:
"You are my nearmost, you who have travelled the farthest,
And you are my constant, who have endured all vicissitudes
In the cradle of sea, Fate's hands, and the spinning waters.
The measure of past grief is the measure of present joy.
Your tears, which have dried to Chance, now spring from a secret.
Here time's glass breaks, and the world is transfigured in music."'

So sang the grains of sand, and while they whirled to a pattern
Taliesin took refuge under the unfledged rock.
He could not see in the cave, but groped with his hand,
And the rock he touched was the socket of all men's eyes,
And he touched the spring of vision. He had the mind of a fish
That moment. He knew the glitter of scale and fin.
He touched the pin of pivotal space, and he saw
One sandgrain balance the ages' cumulus cloud.

from *Cypress and Acacia* (1959)   31

Earth's shadow hung. Taliesin said: 'The penumbra of history is
                                                    terrible.
Life changes, breaks, scatters. There is no sheet-anchor.
Time reigns; yet the kingdom of love is every moment,
Whose citizens do not age in each other's eyes.
In a time of darkness the pattern of life is restored
By men who make all transience seem an illusion
Through inward acts, acts corresponding to music.
Their works of love leave words that do not end in the heart.'

He still held rock. Then three drops fell on his fingers,
And Future and Past converged in a lightning flash:
'It was we who instructed Shakespeare, who fell upon Dante's
                                                    eyes,
Who opened to Blake the Minute Particulars. We are the soul's
                                                    rebirth.'

Taliesin answered: 'I have encountered the irreducible diamond
In the rock. Yet now it is over. Omniscience is not for man.
Christen me, therefore, that my acts in the dark may be just,
And adapt my partial vision to the limitation of time.'

A Man with a Field

If I close my eyes I can see a man with a load of hay
Cross this garden, guiding his wheelbarrow through the copse
To a long, low green-house littered with earthenware, glass and
                                                    clay,
Then prop his scythe near the sycamore to enter it, potted with
                                                    seeds,
And pause where chrysanthemums grow, with tomatoes'
                                                    dragonish beads.
Stooping to fasten the door, he turns on the path which leads
To his rain-pitted bedroom of cellos, and low jugs catching the drops.

If I open my eyes I see this musician-turned-ploughman slow,
Plainly follow his tractor vibrating beneath blue sky,
Or cast his sickle wide, or reach full-length with the hoe,
Or blame the weather that set its blight on a crop or a plan
To mend his roof, or cut back trees where convolvulus ran,
Or attend to as many needs as the holes in a watering-can:
He would wait for the better weather; it had been a wet July.

This year his field lay fallow; he was late putting down his seed.
Cold December concealed with a sighing surplice of snow
His waste of neglected furrows, overgrown with mutinous weed.
Dark, bereaved like the ground, I found him feeble and sick,
And cold, for neither the sticks nor his lamp with a shrunken wick
Would light. He was gone through the wicket. His clock
                                    continued to tick,
But it stopped when the new flakes clustered on an empty room
                                    below.

The Mare

The mare lies down in the grass where the nest of the skylark is
                                    hidden.
Her eyes drink the delicate horizon moving behind the song.
Deep sink the skies, a well of voices. Her sleep is the vessel of
                                    Summer.
That climbing music requires the hidden music at rest.

Her body is utterly given to the light, surrendered in perfect
                                    abandon
To the heaven above her shadow, still as her first-born day.
Softly the wind runs over her. Circling the meadow, her hooves
Rest in a race of daisies, halted where butterflies stand.

Do not pass her too close. It is easy to break the circle
And lose that indolent fullness rounded under the ray
Falling on light-eared grasses your footstep must not yet wake.
It is easy to darken the sun of her unborn foal at play.

from *Cypress and Acacia* (1959)

Hunt's Bay

Hurled, hollow darkness, hungry caves
Where the eye, bending, magnifies
The sea-world, all the imagined graves
Of voices where a tree-log lies:
The centre never is attained;
All is deception, broken-grained.

I have been among broken things,
Picked up the fragile lace
Of a sea-shell though which the wings
Of a gull in a clear blue space
Could be seen, then lost:
By a wave of the sea it was tossed.

Black, tousled weeds,
Bundles of foam, bottles,
Oil, shivering seeds,
Urchins, razorshells, cuttles,
And clouds combed like fleece:
The roar of the sea was peace.

I have walked this beach alone,
I have startled with my praying
The cloven tongue of stone
And seen the white foam straying
Where raven, rock and air
Rock in a dead man's care.

The winds are mad about this time,
Mad the storm's outrageous drum,
Man himself a witless mime
Because the equinoctials come
To snap the needle of his fate,
Tempting his eternal state.

Yet, whether he go or come,
Tossed to the Furies, lost in foam,
Struck by destruction's beak or dumb
Steel, the spirit finds its home.
The raging moon has lost
All conflict with that ghost.

Between the carcase of the tree
And life's imponderable seed,
The mammouth sea-log and the sea
Clutching it with mounting greed,
The creature's truthful husk
Casts out the pagan dust.

Touch you may and touch you can,
White and strange, the drifting wood,
But never touch the severed man
Torn from history for good,
Nailing to splints and spars
Night, and the turning stars.

Trust Darkness

Trust darkness. Dig down
Through earth's crust to no crown.
The surface will moulder
But, tenacious, the root
When you are older
Bring blossom and fruit.

Pull bindweed up first,
That parasite cursed
Which preys on the vision.
From dark root and thorn
In the death of ambition
Let patience be born.

from *Cypress and Acacia* (1959)

On the spade press your foot.
Dig up by the root
Whatever encumbers
Your thought in the grass.
There the seed slumbers,
Cold as dawn was.

Such dancers are seeds,
Each knows what man needs
As it glides from his fingers,
Absently cast.
In their fall lingers
All that is past.

Learn to lie fallow.
Trees naked or yellow
Endure through long Winter
And ride every storm.
Great rewards enter
Where they are born.

No love that fears night
Is fitting and right.
If you seek resurrection
Take root and grow strong.
No bond of affection
Is less than life long.

Hold fast the fine thread
From such bonds that are dead.
Far though you travel
Or stray from that touch,
No hand may unravel
Or teach you as much.

The dead earn their living
By holy forgiving.
No upland or meadow
Where the light flies
But draws from the shadow
Of death-disturbed eyes.

Time begins and time ends
In the meeting of friends.
To deny the occasion
Or count up its cost
Is to mock at the passion
Where nothing is lost.

The Exacting Ghost

I speak of an exacting ghost,
And if the world distrust my theme
I answer: This that moved me most
Was first a vision, then a dream.

By the new year you set great store.
The leaves have turned, and some are shed.
A sacred, moving metaphor
Is living in my mind, though dead.

I would have counted good years more,
But all is changed: your life has set.
I praise that living metaphor
And when I sleep I see it yet.

Why is it, though the conscious mind
Toils, the identity to keep
Forgetful ages leave behind,
No likeness matches that of sleep?

Last night, when sleep gave back the power
To see what nature had withdrawn,
I saw, corrected by that hour,
All likenesses the mind had drawn.

from *Cypress and Acacia* (1959)

In crowded tavern you I found
Conversing there, yet knew you dead.
This was no ghost. When you turned round,
It was indeed your living head.

Time had returned, and pregnant wit
Lodged in your eyes. What health was this?
Never had context been so fit
To give old words new emphasis.

If hope was then restrained by doubt
Or joy by fear, I cannot tell.
All the disturbances of thought
Hung on my words; yet all seemed well.

You smiled. Your reassurance gave
My doubt its death, my hope its due.
I had always known beyond the grave,
I said, all would be well with you.

You fixed contracted, narrowing eyes
To challenge my instinctive sense.
The uncertainty of my surmise
Their penetration made intense.

'What right had you to know, what right
To arrogate so great a gift?'
I woke, and memory with the light
Brought back a weight I could not lift.

In sleep the dead and living year
Had stood one moment reconciled,
But in the next the accuser's spear
Had sacked the city of the child.

Why is it, though the conscious mind
Toils, the identity to keep
Forgetful years will leave behind,
No likeness matches that of sleep?

The Curlew

Sweet-throated cry, by one no longer heard
Who, more than many, loved the wandering bird,
Unchanged through generations and renewed,
Perpetual child of its own solitude,
The same on rocks and over sea I hear
Return now with his unreturning year.
How swiftly now it flies across the sands,
Image of change unchanging, changing lands
From year to year, yet always found near home
Where waves in sunlight break in restless foam.
Old though the cave is, this outlives the cave,
And the grey pool that shuddered when it gave
The landscape life, reveals where time has grown,
Turning green, slowly forming tears to stone.
The quick light of that cry disturbs the gloom.
It passes now, and rising from its tomb,
Carries remorse across the sea where I
Wait on the shore, still listening to that cry
Which bears a ghostly listening to my own;
Such life is hidden in the ringing stone
That rests, unmatched by any natural thing,
And joins, unheard, the wave-crest and the wing.

Angel and Man

Angel: Day breaks. All sighs are ended.
        The sleep of earth, the long night sleep, is over.
Man: Faint incarnation in the mists of dawn,
        Why do you rouse desires I have laid down
        On this sad field where the world tends her wounded
        And shrouds their limbs whose eyes are shut for ever?
        You are not of this life, but of the days
        Of immaturity when, with upturned eyes,
        I lay awake, a child, expecting miracles.

from *Cypress and Acacia* (1959)   39

I think I waited for a star to fall.
Now it is different, and those early oracles
Have lost that power I in those nights would feel.
Yes, once I thought my dreams had been fulfilled.
I thought I saw, quite early in a field,
The annunciation of the morning star,
And that the world had ended with that light.

Angel: That early moment is come true, though late.
That moment was a prophecy of this.
To me alone was given night's darkest wisdom.
I am the first to learn what is for all.

Man: Do not so look at me, for I am ill.
I would believe you, but I cannot.
Too much is hidden.
I hear your speech, but when your speech has faded
It is the earth that counts, where these men lived.
All these the eyelid buried,
These the rough earth hides,
Where are they, then?

Angel: They are gone to the root of the tree.
Just as the red sun went behind the hill,
They pierced the shadows of imagined rest.

Man: If sighs are ended they should wake now, too.

Angel: They do wake, though your ears are not attuned
To those sunk voices which the ground transfigures.
They are like lightning, or the time in sleep
Circling the earth from which the slow leaf breaks.
They do wake, in the murmur of the leaves.

Man: The leaves made that same sound when they were living
But it was not their voices when they lived,
Nor is it now. Let others be deceived.
I know this for a place where footsteps halted
And where each footstep knocked upon the ground,
Seeking true consolation. Think of this.
Spirits were laid here to whom some were dear,
Who left them, sorrowful. Garments touched the leaves,
And where they passed I understood a language
Breathed in the robe and heard by the dumb ground.
I accept this for my portion. Grief was theirs,
And grief, their lot, is likely to be mine.

Yet in the last, most solitary dark
There lives an equilibrium in the soul
Depending on forgiveness. Grant me this,
And I shall hold truth fast without remorse
Under the turning stars.

The Tributary Seasons

I can discern at last how grew
This tree, so naked and so true.
'Spring was my death; when all is sung,
It was the Autumn made me young.'

      Midwinter: packed with ice the butt,
      Splitting its sides.
      Roots hard as iron; the back door shut.
      Heaped wood a ringing axe divides.
      Sacks on the pipes. No river flows,
      No tap, no spring. A skater goes
      Skimming across the pond. A stone
      Stays on the ice where it is thrown.
      Under a bone a blue-tit swings,
      The keen light glancing on his wings.
      To robins crusts and crumbs are tossed,
      Yellow against the white of frost.
      A quilted world. Glazed mistletoe.
      Spades glint, and sledges glide, on snow.
      Boys scoop it up with tingling hands,
      Steadying the snowman where he stands,
      Numb into dusk. Then holly boughs
      Darken the walls in many a house,
      While moth-flakes pile on wood and ground,
      Muffling the panes, and hide all sound.
          The tree of Winter, Winter's tree:
          Winter a dark, a naked tree.

from *Cypress and Acacia* (1959)

What you have seen you have not known.
Look for it now that Winter's gone.
The Winter stars, the silent king,
The angelic night, give way to Spring.

March into May: the lengthening day
With forward light
Kindles the finches in their play,
Turning their wings in amorous flight.
No star in frost more brightly shines
Than, in white grass, these celandines.
Now sunlight warms and light wind shakes
The unopened blooms. The jonquil breaks
Clean from its sheath. Gold wax and gums
Hold the buds fast. The chestnut comes
First into leaf, its trance-bound hands
Pulled from the shell by silken strands,
Breathless and white. The sap unseen
Climbs the stiff stalk and makes all green.
All timeless coils break through, sublime,
The skins and cerements of time.
What spikenard makes the dark earth sweet?
Life from the hyacinth's winding-sheet
Breathes on the fields, and thrushes sing:
'Earth is our mother. Spring is Spring.'
The tree of Spring, the selfsame tree:
Spring is the green, foretelling tree.

What you have seen you cannot know.
Winter is gone, and Spring will go.
These blossoms falling through long grass
Will fade from swallows' quivering glass.

Now the meridian. Summer glows,
A furnace weighed,
Deep in red rose and burnet rose,
Entranced by its own musk and shade.
Birds sing more softly. Foxgloves keep
Over the hedge a misty sleep.
Gardens are secret in their walls

New Selected Poems

And mountains feel their waterfalls.
Murmuring among thick blooms, the bees
Plunge, and in silence honey seize,
Then bear it droning to their hive
Of light by labour kept alive.
Yet still the toil, where leaves are dense,
Breathes of the Spring's first frankincense.
Butterflies dance in blazing beams.
Great trees are hushed, and still the streams.
On river banks, where boughs serene
Reflect their every shade of green,
Bathers take rest, and bodies come
Naked to peace, and their first home.
     The tree of Summer, Summer's tree,
     Lost in the sleep of Adam's tree.

Might this indeed have been the prime,
That Eden state of lasting time?
Men reap the grain and tend the vine,
Heaping their tributes, bread and wine.

    At last late leaves bright-coloured bring,
    Turning time's keys,
    Those fruits foreshadowed by the Spring.
    Acorns and nuts restore their trees.
    As certain jewels have the power
    To magnetize and guide the hour,
    So seeds before our eyes are strewn
    Fast hidden in the pod's cocoon.
    These die, yet in themselves they keep
    All seasons cradled in their sleep.
    Guarding the lost through calms and storms,
    These are the year's eternal forms,
    An alphabet whose letters all
    Mark out a sacred festival.
    The birth of vision from these urns
    Into whose silence dust returns
    Fills the dense wood. Saint Hubert's rein
    Stops the swift horse; for there again
    A stag between its antlers holds

from *Cypress and Acacia* (1959)

Heaven's unique glory, and the world's.
Tree of beginning, Autumn tree:
Divine imagination's tree.

Moonrise

Dew is falling now: the daylight is spent.
Softly, darkly it gathers: night is at hand.
Our world is changed. Along the remembered land
Each landmark changes, hiding the way we went.
All will be altered soon by the moon's ascent,
Her strangeness melt the dimensions we understand,
Bright waves more loudly break, and bring to the sand
Cold threads of moonlight, shreds of a nomad's tent.

Do not succumb to the lure of strangeness. Trust
Better the scarf you wear than light diffused.
Words that once bound shall bind us when we are dust.
Trust narrow bonds; and when you have refused
The enchanter's dissipation of light and shade,
Tread with my heart that place where worlds are made.

Ode at the Spring Equinox

Gone is the solstice, gone the weaning time
Of lambs. These graze the hard
Ground, and the cliff is charred,
The gorse being burnt where now I climb.
Sparse violets, shivering, break to the low sun.
Life has already, though unseen, begun,
Yet still no sign is given; the shore
Sparkles inanimate in the span
Of headlands. Fossil now and man
Speak of a death which was not here before.

It is man's fault if it is so:
His guilt has brought him low,
And where I climb and cast a shade
I bear the consequence of that,
For the mind's load is great
Which knows what menace hangs on all things made.

Icily keen the wind blows, still from the East
Driving the wrinkled tide.
All's withered on one side.
For twenty days it has not ceased
Thrusting against mankind its edge and hate.
The rock resists, borne on its own dead weight.
There the winged form of a lost age
Is fixed, defying from these rocks
The merciless, cold-eyed equinox,
Set to annihilate life with its blind rage.
I see transposed the living sign
Linking that age to mine,
Words upon obelisk or tree,
Vessels of intricate workmanship
Thrown from a battered ship,
Strewn with the wasteful treasures of the sea.

I mark how savagely the knife-wind blows,
Nailing me to the slope.
Out of this earth what hope
Rises with larks, or what repose
Lives on the sea or moves in seabirds' wings?
The wind starves all things and the seaspray stings
The dried-up grass. How can it serve
The lives of men? Storm bringing wood
For fires and pyres, but never food,
What can it offer but the sea-knife's curve?
And now the incurious goats go past
Crossing this charcoal waste,
Moving from bush to rockhead far below,
Feeding on all that man rejects,
Prophets the hill protects,
Lingering in shade like still unmelted snow.

from *Cypress and Acacia* (1959)   45

Ravens return, that pair, sailing in space
Over my head, great wings:
I have watched their foragings;
And now three-quarters up the face
Of vertical rock they have perched upon a ledge
Where, ragged as a bush or blackthorn hedge,
Their nest hangs, out of reach of wave.
And there the raven cliff's burnt gloom
Matches the fiery wing's charred plume
Pitched above strands from many a sandy cave.
Surely the constant that I seek,
Though every hope should break,
Is balanced, hoisted to that rock's
Dangerous height, the uplifted order
Safe from the track of murder,
The streaking, vanishing form of the red fox.

Ruffled with radiance now the black silk wings
Float out, and from this verge
I see them drop, then merge
Wind's desolation, broken things,
With secret life concealed in mottled shells.
I in predicament match them, nothing else.
How could they know as I must know,
These hasards they must overcome
Of whirlwind, thunderstorm and foam,
Are nothing but the shells from which they grow?
All is so hung that harmony,
Though pitched precariously,
Conquers uncertainty, remorse
And every flickering shaft of doubt
When the pure gift flies out
And wonder, like a spring, renews its force.

I watch, and feel the pulse of turning Earth
Now, in the forespring time,
And mark that power sublime
Which makes the passing moment worth
All unformed years lacking this present form.
See, they return, riding both sea and storm.

These they have overcome, but man,
Seizing the blind stone ignorance flings,
Himself can break this chain of wings
And, aiming, maim the loom where life began.
The immediate presence of that fear
Brings distant ages near.
Never let it be said that he,
Despising his own intellect,
Art and his whole Past wrecked,
And cast his planet's faith beneath the sea.

Good Friday

After the winter solstice came
Ice and low flame,
The cockerel step by which the light
Shortened the sleep of earth and night.

And slowly as the days of Lent
Waxed and were spent,
Trees, birds and flowers all increased
In expectation of the feast.

Spring with such promise did abound
That the gemmed ground
Already showed in clustered grass
The printless light of unseen stars.

But now light grows where rays decline.
Now the crushed wine
Transfigures all, leaf, blossom, fruit,
By reference to the sacred root.

Day must die here that day may break.
Time must forsake
Time, and this moment be preferred
To any copy, light or word.

from *Cypress and Acacia* (1959)   47

In this a night we apprehend
Which has no end.
Day dies. We make our choice, and say:
'This, this we seek; no second day.'

Not in the speculative skies
Instruction lies,
But in the nails of darkness driven
Into these hands which hold up heaven.

For, as old ages antedate
Love's present weight,
So the pulse falling gives the chain
Momentum to what years remain.

All lives, to flourish, here should stop
Still; and all hope
To live, must die here first, and pull
New ages to this mountain skull.

Now let the geography of lands
Learn from these hands,
And from these feet the unresting seas
Take, from unfathomed grief, their ease.

Our mortal life is composite
Until we knit
All possible days to this, and make
A seal, from which true day must break.

Come, Easter, come: I was afraid
Your star had strayed.
It was behind our darkest fears
Which could not see their God for tears.

Great Nights Returning

Great nights returning, midnight's constellations
Gather from groundfrost that unnatural brilliance.
Night now transfigures, walking in the starred ways,
Tears for the living.

Earth now takes back the secret of her changes.
All the wood's dropped leaves listen to your footfall.
Night has no tears, no sound among the branches;
Stopped is the swift stream.

Spirits were joined when hazel leaves were falling.
Then the stream hurrying told of separation.
This is the fires' world, and the voice of Autumn
Stilled by the death-wand.

Under your heels the icy breath of Winter
Hardens all roots. The Leonids are flying.
Now the crisp stars, the circle of beginning;
Death, birth, united.

Nothing declines here. Energy is fire-born.
Twigs catch like stars or serve for your divining.
Lean down and hear the subterranean water
Crossed by the quick dead.

Now the soul knows the fire that first composed it
Sinks not with time but is renewed hereafter.
Death cannot steal the light which love has kindled
Nor the years change it.

from *Cypress and Acacia* (1959)   49

from
Affinities
(1962)

The Precision of the Wheel

to my son

How like a wheel of prayer
The year returns,
Precision plucked from air;
And the soul learns
The rustling of those trees,
The changing sound,
Music of cypresses
In hallowed ground
And of that younger green
Which drops its blooms
Sudden as swallows, seen
When April comes.

Your birthday; and, that night,
I stopped, to bind
What I had come to write.
That month my mind
Had run upon a coil
Where light newborn
Revealed in weaver's toil
Lady and unicorn.
The sixfold tapestry
In my mind's eye
Held darkness searchingly;
And then your cry.

Twelve years since then have passed,
And to the day
This verse arrives, my last;
And I must pray,
If on the door I knock
That hides so many dead,
That savagery on rock
In vain be shed.
A secret law contrives
To give time symmetry:
There is, within our lives,
An exact mystery.

From this October night
May you be given
Peace, though the trees by blight
Or storms are riven.
And though the abounding spray
Destroy what issues from it,
May time that law obey,
Strict as a comet,
Which gives in gratitude
All we give, back,
By that rich love renewed
Which misers lack.

Child, what would I not give
To change for you
The world in which we live
And make it new,
Not in the paths and towers
Of prayer and praise,
But in the outrageous powers
Their waste displays.
May night's twin mysteries,
Time's equipoise,
Call upon love, and these
Build all your joys.

from *Affinities* (1962)   51

The Interval

This now being finished and the next unknown,
I must wait long to find the words I need.
Verse tests the very marrow in the bone,
Yet man, being once engaged by song, is freed:
The act itself is prayer, deliberate in its speed.

Nature needs waste; even friendship needs a gap.
Wines love delay and boats a measured stroke.
Distance divides lightning and thunderclap,
Yet time can in a crystal cleared of smoke
Show Earth's arrested lives in mute, transparent cloak.

Now by what current is the swimmer borne
Feeling its pull and subterranean force?
Are the dead parched, or hunger the unborn
For present music, that its certain course
Alone may fill their need and heal them of remorse?

No pressure from this upper ground compels.
It is that dark source which makes all things new
Scoops out, with changing lights, those fragile shells
Whose voice would perish, did I not pursue
Their inmost labyrinth still, to give the god his due.

Rewards of the Fountain

Let the world offer what it will,
Its bargains I refuse.
Those it rewards are greedy still.
I serve a stricter Muse.

She bears no treasure but the sands,
No bounty but the sea's.
The fountain falls on empty hands.
She only gives to these.

The living water sings through her
Whose eyes are fixed on stone.
My strength is from the sepulchre
Where time is overthrown.

If once I labour to possess
A gift that is not hers,
The more I gain in time, the less
I triumph in the verse.

Vine

Deep-rooted vine, delay your fruit
Beyond youth's rashness. I have seen
Rich promise wither to the root
Before its time had been.

Drain all the darkness of the soil
And stand there shrivelled, crisp and dry,
Too lifeless in your parchment coil
To open one green eye.

Some watch the March winds animate
Those early bulbs in Winter's bed.
Envy them not, but keep your state.
Let others think you dead.

Contain in secrecy that balm
Strengthening the sap before it move,
That the broad leaves from wells of calm
One day grow dark with love.

I know a tree as dry as yours.
The patient leaf is put forth late.
Its life is anchored in the hours
For which the heart must wait.

from *Affinities* (1962)

Affinities

I find them in the wings of every age
While fools and rhetoricians hold the stage.

They know instinctively that speculation
Will never reach a single true equation.

There is no theory, however strict,
A work of genius cannot contradict.

Who pulls tradition down and sets up fashion?
Pretence is one thing, and another, passion.

In every smith whose work I come across
Tradition is the ore, fashion the dross.

They who skim ice cannot afford to stumble;
If pausing they went through, they might grow humble.

Pretenders mock the dead to make their mark,
As little children shout who fear the dark.

'His work is new. Why then, his name encumber
With ancient poets?' He is of their number.

Complain against the dead, but do not sue.
They never read you, much less injured you.

Must it be anarchy to love that nation
Which counts among its assets inspiration?

from *The Childhood of Hölderlin*

'Only one Summer grant, you Powerful Ones,
    And one Autumn to my full-ripened song,
That my heart willingly by the tender
    Harp-strings be satisfied; let me die, then.

The soul to which its godlike right when alive
    Came not, down in Orcus shall find no rest;
But once the holy one that against
    My heart lies close, the poem, is uttered,

Welcome, then, O peace of the world of Shades!
    Content am I, even if the play of strings
Has not down-guided my footsteps; once
    Lived I as gods live, and more I crave not.'

            'To the Fates' – Hölderlin

2

He came, like love, to beseeching strings. Before birth
He had experienced death. He sang in the cradle.
He knew the tenderest fire in eyes declined
Where his mother leaned. Then, racing out in the fields,
True friends he found: the mountains were his companions.
At dusk the rivers returned to the edge of the eyes.
He touched the stars, the wind, the crowns of the reeds.

If he lingered late, he felt the sigh of the dew
Like souls found late upon Lethe. In purest darkness
His eyes shone with tears. He thought of the underworld.
He grew in stature. He felt the arms of the gods
About him. When people spoke, he remained confused.
If he touched a bud, he knew the secrets of nature.
The Rhine, the demi-god, thundered, a Titan in chains.

At evening he would return by a wooded path
To his mother's house where myths of the Greeks were stored.
His eyes marvelled, reading the deeds of heroes.
At night, when his book was closed, the curtain stirred,
Pure gold in the rising moon; and he saw the valleys
Transformed with unearthly light. He acclaimed his kindred.
Quite still, he smiled, caught up to the plains of heaven.

'Holy dawn, the man who is not a hero
Does not see you; therefore you are not honoured,
Beautiful sun-god; therefore your lyre is silent,
Except where pious peoples watch you ascend.
You are too still for the eyes of men; your music
Rises solemn, not knowing trouble or care,
In perfect praise, much brighter than any dream.

I have known and loved you, Aether, better than men.
Late, when moonlight bathed the enchanted fields,
When the last notes of the sun-youth's lyre had faded
Leaving the listening mountains lost in music,
I have seen them walk, in airs of the gods, those genii,
Patient as stars. My tongue is the tomb of angels.
My words are silence. Orpheus plays to the Shades.'

Yet nearer the bone were his words on the master of tragedy,
After the sun-god's music, this upon Sophocles:
'Many attempted in vain, through joy, the most joyful to utter;
Here, at last, I am held: here, in the tragic, it speaks.'

5

The pine moves. Like an instrument it responds
To the music of Earth. It drinks the life of the underworld.
The pine-cone falls, rolls, rain-sodden, at rest.
Under the rock thunders, remorseless, the waterfall,
And trampled, year upon year, by confused horses,
The violet-root secretes the breath of the century.

New Selected Poems

Poet of rivers and supernatural love,
His crime was tenderness. Goethe was reigning in Weimar,
Holding, majestic, his court, like a classical sun.
For Hölderlin Schiller surpassed him, the last of the Hellenes,
An unapproachable star. Yet neither accepted
Their eccentric visitor, pledged to a loftier myth.

Acclaiming creation hung on the word of God,
His was the hardest task, his lot to be spurned;
And yet his fragments outshine their accomplished works.
The living universe moves in the final hymns.
The measure, there, is the deepest measure of thought,
Sprung from the purest love, for love is the measure.

'The beginning of riches is truly', he said, 'in the sea',
Springing from dissolution, the dazzling one
Casting up shells, out of its boisterous movement
Casting up Greece, the light of perfect meanings,
The shape of perfect statues, that are still:
How soon the tumultuous waters make all nothing.

Terrible destinies sleep in the shadow of calm.
The prophets of order suffer on harmony's wheel
The tension between their vision and that which exists.
Involved in the sun, the language of petals and leaves
His mother tongue, he saw, as one blind, by miracle
Given true sight, divinity's earth-born day.

And late, remembering the mountains and the Dordogne,
His eyes fixed in thought on the tumbling river,
He wrote, at the end of the Andenken:
                                        'Great as a sea,
The river goes out. The sea, though,
Takes and gives recollection,
And love, too, fastens the eyes intently.
What endures, however, poets create.'

from *Affinities* (1962)   57

6

He saw Dionysus clear from the forge of Vulcan,
Birthplace of wonders, flash of the deathless moment.
For who could train down with such grace the intuitive lightning
To the thunderous chains of his cloud? The courses of rivers
Remained a compelling mystery; yet when he wrote
Of these, he no longer watched, he *became* the river.
So swift his thought, so close to the life he saw,
He knew the rose as the rose is known to herself,
Fell with the cataract's fall, or became that eagle
Of piercing sight, or learnt the time of the fig-tree,
Not by time, but by breast-feather and leaf.

8

But now it was late.
The sands were chill, no comfort in earth, and in air
The bird of night which hovered before his eyes
In premonition of exile, herald of fate,
Left him now, to return when the hour of death
Closed his lips on an incomprehensible prayer.
In the room where he passed his days his book lay open,
But the verses he made in age were formal and simple;
He scattered some on the stream from the tree of his tower,
Like leaves of acceptance, tranquil in thought and rhyme.
Long he lived there, a stranger to his own name,
Entranced with landscape, smiling over the Neckar,
Dying beyond his time.

9

If there could be
A second genesis of the first Adam,
His mind fixed on the all-creating God,
A child to the mother raised, his eyes remaining
Full of that first pure concord, light with light,
Adam redeemed, both Heaven and Earth at once
Mirrored in eyes, proportioning the limbs,
The mountains moving in their primal shape
In dew and worship, cities and their rivers
Moving in harmony with that first music,
Hölderlin's dream would live.
                              But now he speaks
In fragmentary language
Of castles built by the heavenly ones; man as demi-god,
And a world huger, torn in fragments, glory
Accessible only to faith, miraculous bridges,
Visions too great for man without the cadence
And broken utterance of our elected guide.

And still through darkness, Nazareth, Capernaum;
The hymn to the Madonna;
Holy vibrations of unbounded joy
Still sounding from the deepest hour of man,
Grief keeping pace with joy.
Still, since the great wrong and the wrong redeemed,
To live would be to suffer, from that hour.

Because his song was pure false tongues are silent.
Through him the dead speak, and the quick are changed.

from *Affinities* (1962)

Bishopston Stream

River last seen in Spring, you race in the light of Autumn.
Now, as you run through hazels, their leaves are already falling.
Out of the wood I come, astonished again to find you
Younger and swifter.

There were two voices then, moving about in foliage.
One called the other voice, then a great bird made silence.
This was their meeting-place, here where the heron paddling
Stepped on the square stone.

Crossing an open space, haunted in June by mayflies,
Into the gloom of trees you wind through Bishopston Valley,
Darting, kingfisher-blue, carrying a streak of silver
Fished from oblivion.

Over your tunnelled song, pulled in the year's declining,
Lies an uprooted elm, struck by a gale or lightning.
Trout in the shadows hide; black is the hurrying water,
Thronged once with Spring stars.

May not the two I saw be in this hour united
Who are gone different ways? Water, that young Rebecca,
Naomi, Ruth, once heard, voices above a pitcher,
Late let me stoop here.

Yet if I listen closely, singing of separation,
Singing of night you go, through a continual darkness,
River of exile's voice, harps that were hung heard plainly
Now, in the clear dusk.

Even by day you run through a continual darkness.
Could we interpret time, we should be like the angels.
Always against your sound there is a second river
Speaks, by its silence.

Music of Colours:
Dragonfoil and the Furnace of Colours

1

Bright petal, dragonfoil, springing from the hot grass,
Dazzling profusion continually fading,
Sprung from the white fire, tiger-lily, snake-fang
Basking in brilliance; deep in fume of poppies
Sleep the black stamens.

Where were these born then, nurtured of the white light?
Dragonfly, kingfisher breaking from the white bones,
Snows never seen, nor blackthorn boughs in winter,
Lit by what brand of a perpetual summer,
These and the field flowers?

All is entranced here, mazed amid the wheatfield
Mustardseed, chicory, sky of the cornflower
Deepening in sunlight, singing of the reapers,
Music of colours swaying in the light breeze,
Flame wind of poppies.

Lizards on dry stone; gipsy-bright nasturtiums
Burning through round leaves, twining out in torch-buds;
Even the stream's tongue alters where the rose-blaze
Hangs in forgetfulness. Who beneath the water
Plucks at the dark strings?

Where is the young Spring, clustered myosotis?
Have you forgotten, drugged beneath the heat haze,
White stems of bluebells hidden in the dark wood,
Swan of the lily, purple-throated iris,
Lost in your silence?

Speak: what Ophelia lies among your shadows?
Is it her music, or is it Eurydice
Gone from your bank, for there a spirit's absence
Wakens the music that was heard by Orpheus,
Lost, where the stream glides.

from *Affinities* (1962)

Far off, continually, I can hear the breakers
Falling, destroying, secret, while the rainbow,
Flying in spray, perpetuates the white light,
Ocean, kindler of us, mover and mother,
Constantly changing.

2

Brand lit in foliage, in the heart of summer,
Breaking from the live coals, torn from the seed-pod,
Flaunting its brilliance, petals of the burnet-rose
Stirred by a slow wind, under gold antennae
Wasp-gold, simmering, hovering in heat haze,
Red silk of poppies:

June wakes the music that was known to Orpheus,
Breathed by the fire-god, muted for enchantment,
Fire-misted marigold, clustered myosotis
Sprung to remember the river's lamentation,
June flowers hiding the footprints of Eurydice
Seized by the dark king.

Yet the turf tells me: she it is, no other,
Touches the rose-blaze, gathers what became her
Music. Forgetfulness holds her like a girdle
Silent. Only by absence is the song made
Audible. Orpheus, leaning above Lethe,
Knows every note there.

There the stream flies on to its own beginning,
Slips through the fresh banks, woods of their escaping,
Leaving in glory patterns of a lost world,
Leaves that are shadows of a different order,
Light, born of white light, broken by the wave's plunge
Here into colours.

Ocean, kindler of us, mover and mother,
Assailing the rock with variety of music,
Inconstancy of pattern, eternally renewing
Through mother-of-pearl the colours of destruction
Dissolving, lost in the whisper of the sea-cave,
Sigh of a gull's wings!

Here now is summer, this perennial wonder
Of fireborn blossoms, the sudden incarnation
True for this moment, therefore never dying,
Never transfigured by the net of sunbeams,
Being of the spray, the rainbow from the breakers,
Born, like the white girl.

3

Who half asleep, or waking, does not hear it,
Drone where the bees swarm, sky of the cornflower,
Blaze of a water-lily, music of the reapers,
Lithe bodies moving continually forward
Under the heat haze?

Dust drops from campions where the hedge is hottest.
Foxgloves and grasses tremble where a snake basks,
Coiled under brilliance. Petals of the burnet-rose
Flash there, pulsating: do the gold antennae
Feel for the white light?

All that is made here hides another making;
Even this water shows a magic surface.
Sky is translated; dragonfly and iris
Rise from the grey sheath; unremembered shadows
Cling, where the bloom breaks.

Yet, not that bloom, not any kind of foliage,
Cup, sheath or daystar, bright above the water,
Clustered forgetmenots tufted on the stream's bank,
Not one recalls the virginals of April
Heard, when the wood grieved.

from *Affinities* (1962)   63

Waking entranced, we cannot see that other
Order of colours moving in the white light.
Time is for us transfigured into colours
Known and remembered from an earlier summer,
Or into breakers

Falling on gold sand, bringing all to nothing.
Fire of the struck brand hides beneath the white spray.
All life begins there, scattered by the rainbow;
Yes, and the field flowers, these deceptive blossoms,
Break from the furnace.

Five Poems of Magdalenian Darkness

1. Touch

Never such rest I had
As before I drew breath.
Here I lie on the bed
At the point of death,
I, the Magdalen, dead
In all but faith.

Now the sorrow I lived
Is taken away.
Death now calls for the gift
And I must obey.
Joy is the certainty left:
Do not delay.

Many shall murmur of me:
'I have known such,
Fickle and bright as the sea,
Gave herself much.'
Broken at last though I be,
Truth is in touch.

2. *The Stair*

Bitter my life has been, not sweet,
Yet grief has made me strong.
Was ever vision more complete
Or hope more plainly hung
Than when with tears I washed His feet
Whose body paid for wrong?

Darkness, compel that hour to stay
Whose pledge is in the tomb.
The leper's praises die away.
How silent is the room.
All is remembered from the day,
And still death will not come.

These seconds wait upon the crime
None but the dead can bear,
But I renounce unholy time
And that sweet morning air.
Down through derision He did climb:
I choose the bitter stair.

3. *The Music of Justice*

Death, I know you already: you come to take what I have.
Poor though you think me and frail, in this darkness by which I
                                                   am blest,
Never so rich was I yet as now at the edge of the grave.
Of all the sweet joys I have looked for, this is the dearest and best.
I, that was love's anointer, am ready to die as a slave.
Make me whole with the music of justice, and hide what has
                                                robbed me of rest.

from *Affinities* (1962)

4. *The Knockers*

Older in sorrows and years
Than the girl I was then,
I remember in darkness the spears,
Low voices of men.
That knocking that fell on my ears,
I hear it again.

Run, spirits, and find in your track
All the days that I spent.
Take the joy I would willingly lack.
Leave me broken or bent,
But inspire me to drive the mob back
Or curb their intent.

In starlight the legions are come.
Northward they move,
Leaving one dead in each home,
As when there drove
Spears from that Herod, now Rome
Fearing His love.

5. *The Anointing*

Hour of anointing, dear life, how near you are now it is late.
My heart beats: it is stronger than death that takes it away.
There are footsteps again in the courtyard: I can hear the
conspirators wait.
How still the room; and the stars of midnight stay.

Where now are the many companions I met in the field or the road?
When reaping was done, or the treading of grapes, they came for
delight.
Yet beyond the grave One drew them. To whom is my last breath
owed?
I touched, I anointed His feet, on the threshold of night.

New Selected Poems

And where are the many He cleansed, the lepers, the lame and
                                                    the blind?
A new generation has risen. They are come who did not know Him.
Tell them that this is the room the strong must infallibly find,
Their vigour kindled and fed by the love they owe Him.

Returning from Harvest

It is always so: the declining
Daylight touching the edge
Of a window quickens knowledge,
Whets the invisible wing

Of thought, as the mist-hazed hummer
Michaelmas patterns weaves.
The stream understands the leaves
Better than in high summer.

And however the intellect
Predict the pattern of days,
It is never repeated. Always
A change we did not expect

Interprets the sickle gleaning
High sheaves for a sheltered place.
A young moon hangs in space
But shines with a different meaning.

Evening never deceives
Man, as the waggon swings
Back from migrating wings
To his mud-encrusted eaves.

They are gone before the stoat
In the iron track dawn-fires smelt
Changes his chestnut pelt
For the white of the ermine's coat.

from *Affinities* (1962)   67

O freshness of the precise
Season, frost-clear sky,
Full harvest tilted high
In the ruts of tomorrow's ice.

from
Fidelities
(1968)

Two Sources of Life

The time we measure and the time we know
Move in the branches drinking life, the giver.
Being young, we bathed here, and shook off the river,
Then stood above the stream and watched it flow.
An image in the water shone below,
Armed with a secret we could not deliver.
Those beams were like the arrows in a quiver
For which our expectation was the bow.

But ask: when was it that the current took us
So deeply into life that time forsook us,
Leaving us nothing but the need to give?
We were transfigured by the deaths of others.
That was the spring, when first we knew our brothers
And died into the truth which made us live.

Earth and Fire

All do not seek the exalted fire;
All do not let the moment bless.
And yet, what so rewards desire,
So nourishes? Confess:
He's wrong who toils for less.

Measure the ground and weigh its yield,
Changing the crops while seasons turn.
Yet who can say a barren field
Where the dry brambles burn
Brings not the best return?

Then the fine breath of wintry air
Answers the crisp and stubborn earth.
Without the exaltation there
Uniting death and birth,
What is a man's song worth?

Earth's natural order brings a wealth
Of promise, bounty, and regret.
Through changes he alone has health
And writes off all the debt
Whose heart on heaven is set.

The Sibyl

While kings rode forth to conquest I stayed here.
The shadows of their laurels crossed my wall.
While heroes came to terms with their own fear,
They did not know I should outlast them all.
Whether men called me wanton or austere,
My cave became their common port of call:
How many left me, chastened by the tear
Which knew their destiny, but would not fall.

And still my vision knows behind the bone
To separate their lives and set them free.
I hold from heaven the power to see what's gone
So clearly, that what is or is to be
Hinders no whit the noblest I have known,
His passion rooted, singing like a tree.

The Guest

All day, all night, wind and wild rain had blown;
Then the gale dropped, and in September weather
Where sunlight lingered on the pulse of stone
Red thistle and wild harebell shone together.

The cliff's crossed paths lay silvered with slug tracks
Where webs of hanging raindrops caught the sun.
A thrush with snail cocked sideways like an axe
Knocked with quick beak to crack it on a stone.

Stumbling, a blue-black beetle groped its way
Where crickets perched and dropped like jewelry.
Dawn's pestle mixed fresh colours for the day,
And, far beneath, a cormorant crossed the sea.

There was no guest to watch the landscape change.
All day slow, silken threads gold spiders spun.
Towards evening then I broke them, seeing a strange
Fleece in low heather catch the western sun.

There, halfway down the cliff, in fallen flight
I came on plumage, tufted claws, wide wings,
A white owl dead, feeding fritillary light
Into those roots from which the heather springs.

No wound appeared, though death had shrunk the eyes.
The bright wings held no marking but their own.
How close it lay no mouse dared recognize,
Lest it should pounce, and tear it to the bone.

from *Fidelities* (1968)

The Razor Shell

I am the long lean razor shell:
Do not interpret me too soon.
Streak of the wind with tawny stains,
The sky's quill-feather marked my grooves,
The sea is hidden in my veins.
I am a part of all that moves,
And more than this, of what remains.
Here on the sand in burning noon
I lie, forgotten by the swell.
I hear the breakers and the oars
Falling along the level shores
And beating down the golden grains.
Let Solomon consider well
And take me cool into his hand,
Then ask, before he count the sand:
What is that labour to the moon?

Fisherman

I learn, as my fingers mend the net, what none without nets can
                                                            know.
The sun of that knowledge flickers within. It is not the knotting
                                                        of cords;
It is not the silent pull on the net, the pull of the sea, when the flow
Carries the weight of an unknown tide, when the heart is laden
                                                    with words.

How many tides have ebbed and flowed where pebble and
                                                broken shell
Shine in a tumbled spangle of weed: O little weights of the mind,
O little floats to carry me up in a moment none can foretell,
We are taken, each, by the task we choose, by the net our hands
                                                        designed.

New Selected Poems

There are silver fish that flash before day, in the fragile moment
of dawn.
I have seen them shiver before my eyes, then vanish before light
shone.
I know the weight of unspoken words, of speech that cannot be
drawn.
I crouch, and my life returns to the sea. It trembles, then it is gone.

Cornfields

Corn waves in the wind:
A sigh, early and late.
The eye of the barley is blind
When the stalk is stiff and straight.

Ears, ripening, rise,
Then gold, heavily fall;
The breath of nativity sighs:
The star is laid in the stall.

Learn, learn of the corn
Of things coming to pass,
Of wings, and a foal unborn
To the mare asleep in the grass.

Crest follows on crest;
A sigh moving in air,
A rustling of wings in the nest
Ascends from the dreaming mare.

Birth's tremor within
The fruit earth has concealed,
Does it summon life to begin
And the sun to reap the field,

Joy weighing at dusk
The scales, heavy and light,
The balance of ear and husk,
Daybreak dreaming of night?

from *Fidelities* (1968)

Trees in a Town

Why must they fell two chestnuts on the road?
I did not see the lorry and its load
Before a wall had grown where they had stood.
I wish I thought that sphinxlike block was good
Builders have raised, to brood upon the loss
Of those two chestnuts where the two roads cross.
In spite of all the gain some say has been,
How can my eyes accept the altered scene?
How often, checked here on my way to work
By the instant luck of life, I saw themes fork
Into the boughs, where thought could learn as much
As sight will learn, till it is taught by touch.
In March abounding sunlight drenched the tree,
But still those sticky buds would not set free
Their secret fledgling silk of crumpled fronds
Held in the icy trance of winter's bonds.
Summer's wide green brought gloom where eyes could range
Up the dark foliage of attentive change;
But soon that gloom was battered by a squall,
Then the long, yellow leaves were first to fall.

After, in a frost, when all the boughs were bare,
What sudden grace the trees would print on air.
Call either tree a book for men to read
In any season; and then ask what need
A foursquare building had to pull them down.
I can forgive the traffic of this town
Its noise and brutal speed, but only just.
Metal and brick and glass above the dust
Smile on the road and on the lawn between.
What else is there the planners have not seen?
A fig-tree, thick with fruit which never grows
Ripe in our sun. When June is here it throws
Young, yellow fruit to the pavement while, unspent,
The broad leaves thrive and spread a fertile scent,
Warm memory of abundant nature's loins.
The shrivelled figs grow hard as ringing coins,

Seeming to prove the toll-gate has been paid
Out of that garden to the builder's trade.
How patient is the shadow those leaves cast:
They rob the Present who despoil the Past;
In all Utility's cold eye has seen
Beauty's profusion yields to what is mean,
And yet a fallen leaf can still express
Man's exile, his lost innocence, his dress.

Trees in a town, how long will they survive
The merchant's axe for all that looks alive?
How shall miraculous blossom, leaf and seed
Breathe life into the body lulled by speed,
Racing to nothing in an asphalt place?
Something is lost. The trees' obstructive grace
Seems to slick progress wasteful and obscene,
Whose highway must be useful and be clean.

Sonnet

The prose purveyors of doubt, the dismantlers of
Ecstasy, who traffic without a god
In broken metre, would have their Pegasus shod
With discord, not strict numbers. At love they scoff,
And then, in the revolution of anti-love,
Unsheathe chaos, the death of the period,
While a new Sibyl, shrieking above her tripod,
Proclaims transformation, treachery, trough.

Yet even the disenchanted, disordered, fret
For lost order. Breakers recall rhyme,
Anchors weighed, and divine proportions set.
As hawk hovers, as compass needle in time
Flies unswerving, steadied, where the stars climb,
Fixed laws hallow what none can forget.

from *Fidelities* (1968)

Rebirth

Just as the will to power
From youth exhausted spins
To earth, it sees a flower
Rooted in ruins.
From that remaking hour
Perception begins.

This for which I care,
By the crowd denied,
Holds a truth so clear,
By none identified.
I would expound it here,
But my tongue is tied.

Dearest things are so:
Neglected, they stay;
Applauded, they go.
The river runs away
And we check its flow
Only when we play.

Strange, that in all we make
A solemn purpose can,
More than most things, break,
While some lesser plan
By accident will wake
The deepest roots in man.

New Selected Poems

The Snow Curlew

Snow has fallen all night
Over the cliff. There are no paths.
All is even and white.
The leaden sea ebbs back, the sky is not yet light.
Hidden from dawn's grey patch
Behind frosted windows, ash ticks out faded hearths.

How quickly time passes. There is no mark
Yet upon this manuscript of snow.
Where water dripped, ice glitters, sheaved and stark.
The pen has fallen from the hand of dark.
White are lintel and latch.
Earth has forgotten where her dead go.

Silence. Then a curlew flutes with its cry
The low distance, that throbbing Spring call,
Swifter than thought. It is good-bye
To all things not beginning and I must try,
Making the driftwood catch,
To coax, where the cry fades, fires which cannot fall.

Means of Protection

As plovers trail their wings
To hide a nest from men's concern,
Right lovers turn
Talk that nears treasured things.

The best of judgment says
No case is won by what speech proves,
Least of all love's.
We live by silences.

from *Fidelities* (1968)

All that is fair courts danger.
When wit with daring lights a face
Of candid grace,
I, the protecting stranger,

Must turn my gaze, for fear
I lose that vision, for the mind
Needs shade, to find
The full light of the sphere.

Such means will fortify
The true from uncouth trespassers
And keep, in verse,
All hushed, till they pass by.

I must, seeing I have fought
Error, both in myself and men,
Build, like the wren,
To understand my thought,

A number of small nests
In branches that may catch the sun,
To guard that one
In which the interest rests.

Vultures

Fling bones to vultures, who dissect
Thoughts of a living man when dead.
Trust the wide wings to spread his shade
And win what he hates most, respect.

The Stayers

When the trees drop their leaves in frost,
Old Earth, deep-rooted, knows her own;
Poets, who loved her, are the last
To leave her, when the rest have flown.

Strictness of Speech

Lord, defend us from the peroration.
Silence all that politicians say.
They who plough us in to make a nation
Have not known the vision we obey.

Wits that learn from mother-wit are keenest,
Nor is there nobility of style
Till the proud man kneels to help the meanest.
They who justify themselves are vile.

Unity of the Stream

Take this into account:
Like water from a fount
Until it reach the sea,
Song is unique delight;
You cannot snap its flight
Like wood across your knee.

You cannot tear apart
The single jet of art
That glitters there entire.
The innocent is bound
To wisdom in the ground
Of that revealing fire.

from *Fidelities* (1968)

Song is all mastery
And first virginity;
Without it time were vain.
It lives to make love fly
Through nuptials of the sky
And feed the earth like rain.

Fidelities

The fountain gathers, in a single jet,
Fidelities where beams together run,
Thrives upon loss, enriches us with debt.

Nothing will match the day's full unison.
I love to see light break; and yet, and yet,
The final arbiter is not the sun.

Bounteous that brother, but he will forget
Others whose eyes the hand of death has closed,
Nor touch, nor seek them, when their light has set.

Seeing of what compound splendour life's composed,
Who could believe it now a part once played,
With so much owing to so many a ghost?

Of love's stern language noblest lives are made.
The shell of speech by many a voice is shot
Whose light, once kindled, cannot be betrayed.

A certain cadence underlies the plot;
However fatally the thread is spun,
The dying man can rise above his lot.

For me neglect and world-wide fame were one.
I was concerned with those the world forgot,
In the tale's ending saw its life begun;

And I was with them still when time was not.

New Selected Poems

To a Shell

At last, beautiful shell,
Lie there crushed; but the sea
Cannot obliterate yet
Faith I remember well:
A house facing the sea.
Hard and bitterly
Though waves beat on that wall
From the swirling quicksands of debt,
I swear that it cannot fall.

Nor can you drag those words,
Confident in their day,
Down to the unknown deep.
I have a net whose cords
Gather the fallen day
And make the forgotten stay
In all but the detail death
Moves to the realm of sleep,
So strong is the pledge of breath.

And though the magical dice,
Loaded for nothing, toss
All to perdition, left
In darkness, held in a vice,
No white breaker can toss
All to a total loss.
Still the relic will hold,
Caught in a secret cleft,
Tenderer light than gold.

All I remember, all
Of the locked, unfolding days
Where to-morrow's treasure shines.
Fragile nautilus caul,
Tell the fingers of days:
'Find me. Enter the praise
Of Eden's morning, inlaid
With dazzling, intimate lines.
Touch, and the world will fade.'

The Beaver

The violent praise the destructive rites of the hawk;
A kingly deceit has the snake,
Vigilant, sinuous in leaves,
Coiled in a pattern of envy,
With a tongue of venom.

Deep forests protect the weak and provoke the strong.
Like a tree, antlers spring
From the velvet head of the elk.
Wolves hunt in a pack.
Ferocious bears have their cave in rock,

I would impose a form on the barbarous wilderness.
I do not trust the trees.
I trust my own teeth
To move them to my design
Away from this carpentry of death.

Flying out of the sunset, stiff, petalled lilies to pluck,
Flamingoes alight on the lake.
I study their stilted reflection.
At dawn they are gone.
In the reeds, the industrious moorhen,

So early building a nest where those fires were banked,
Knows already by instinct
How high, when the long rains come,
The water will flood, whose calm
Shall make the unwary succumb.

This benevolent water deceives who will not use it.
It speaks in my language, tacit.
In a climate of fear and conflict,
A secret architect,
I carry the plans of the city.

I construct where hostile conditions hold others in bondage.
I fell, and measure to usage,
Turning the course of the river,
Dragging logs of my labour
To uphold the measure of life.

Against wild nature I set the cool and Athenian;
A metrical city is mine:
Lanes in harmony laid
From the central beat of the blood.
I do not sprawl. I saw to the level of need.

Triads

Who am I to load the year with continual misunderstanding?
I will not accuse winter of a protracted hardness,
Nor spring of callousness, nor summer of regret.

The oak-leaf changes: green gloss cups the acorn.
First hidden, then emerging from resistance to statement,
The fruit holds nothing in its fullness but the tree.

To have held through hail, stormwinds, and black frost in darkness
Through the long months, gives meaning to the bud when it opens.
Song loses nothing of moments that are past.

So my labour is still: it is still determination
To resolve itself slowly in the weathers of knowledge.
By virtue of the hidden the poem is revealed.

Remember Earth's triads: the faith of a dumb animal,
The mountain stream falling, music to the wheat-ears;
The salt wave echoing the grieving of the bones.

The lamb leaps: it is stubborn in its innocence.
The hawk drops, in the energy of instinct.
Dawn fires kindle perfection like a sword.

from *Fidelities* (1968)   83

Fire: the hawk's talons, the tongue of the chameleon,
In a peacock's wings' lightning the contraction of glory,
In death the last miracle, the unconditional gift.

What do I need but patience before the unpredictable,
The endurance of the stepping-stone before the footprint,
Cadence that reconciles wisdom and the dance?

I need more, I need more. In the moment of perception
Fit me, prayer, to lose everything, that nothing may be lost.
The stone that accumulates history is falling.

History is a pageant, and all men belong to it.
We die into each other: remember how many
Confided their love, not in vain, to the same earth.

Air

If a man have but one string,
One, on which to play,
Or in all the world one thing
He alone can say,

Let him turn to other kinds,
Lose and find himself,
Find the peace another finds,
Never for himself.

Music is of music wrought,
Silent though it stay.
Stretch the string away from thought
And the string will play.

Second Air

After all is said,
Then the words alone
Keep a single thread,
Yes, one tone.

Perfect music is
What it had to be:
Wit, the gift of grace,
Bound, yet free.

Everything is caught,
Singular and glad;
Then the after-thought,
Though not sad,

Leads us to a plain
Where the stream is dry,
And we hear again
That low sigh

Earth has breathed who hears
After all is said,
One with many tears
Still unshed.

The Coin

Taste the coin beneath your tongue;
Then the song is rightly sung.

Never shall the fountain leap
Till you come to terms with sleep.

For who knows the worth of breath
Till he measures it by Death?

Then the athletic body is
Made aware of witnesses.

Every ripple on the sea
Has a secret voice and key.

Think how many went before
Then you understand the shore.

Then your cadence will be true,
Balanced by the jet it threw.

Vision, where the fountain fell,
Masters more than time can tell.

Not by reason or by sense
Alone, can words be made intense,

But by this, alive and dead,
Breaking from the fountain-head.

Sage or lover cannot say
Truth in any other way.

Dead and living cannot join
Till your tongue has touched the coin.

from *Uncollected Poems* (1969)

from
The Ballad of the Outer Dark
(1979)

A Dry Prophet

Except for the unreclaimed land
Of wild creatures, birds
And children, he had no planned
Conquest, no territorial dreams.
Cities he did not understand,
Or ways of indulgent thought;
So he picked wry themes,
And finding himself caught
In a cage of fury, he would pluck
The wires, not
For the lyric note struck
But to expose the plot
Of time he tenanted; words were cords
For flagellation, not strings.
How could it be otherwise?
It is in freedom the lark sings.
With his eye for wronged things,
Greed, hypocrisy, lies,
Bitterness fed his words.

Time smouldered in his eyes' furnace
Watching the corruption of days,
A dry prophet, observant –
While the hourglass ran –
Of every false direction
In which life moved.
Say of this man
He was sure in his affection
For the things he loved,
But did not commit his tongue to praise.
Excess of words galled

His instinct. Rather he called
Reticence a truer servant,
More likely to lead to grace.

To judge others
Is to judge ourselves; but he,
Alert to that law
Of merciless scrutiny,
Judged himself first, and saw
Clearly, in a landscape exposed to scorn,
The lines of life on his brothers'
Faces, and his own
Lineaments in theirs, melancholy
Marked there, lines of distress
Leading to judgement slowly,
Traced before he was born.

Rhadamanthus and the New Soul

Admit the new soul from the tethered boat
Where sorrows fly like seabirds seeking bread.
Men are remembered by the words they wrote.
These, not the printless waters, nurse their dread.

'Is it not true, the dead forget their pains?
The pains of others, then, outlast our own.
Too much is gone, too little now remains.
Weep, and efface the writing on the stone.'

In crafts of evil who compares with man?
How many in the death-cells learnt his ways.
What victims could not overcome, I can.
Speak low, for where you walk, another prays.

'I saw too much, and did not wish to live.
My pity ran too deep for time to kill.
Read in my eyes their sorrow, and forgive
Those others who obeyed a tyrant's will.'

from *The Ballad of the Outer Dark* (1979)

Death cannot heal the dead of all their pains.
Life is a tree that blossoms in the stone.
Its root is sacred; every hour it gains
Until at last it masters all that's known.

'Stern judge, you understand us more than I.
Mercy there was, and kindness, in the stream.
I prayed for death, and still I could not die.
My dream still holds me. Wake me from my dream.'

Cast off the tethered boat, while overhead
The starving seabirds cry and veer away.
He is of those whose fingers crushed the bread,
And who can perish, born on Judgment Day?

from
The Breaking of the Wave
(1979)

May You Love Leaves

May you love leaves, complete yet unfulfilled,
Dancing in the light, in the shade where light is stilled.
May the wild woodpecker, knocking on the hollow
Treetrunk remind you, and the voice of the late swallow
That distance is mortal. May you then run complete
Into that circle created by your feet
And may you be astounded, when the rest are gone,
By the chill water splashing on the stone.
Wait, then, for patience is the friend of love,
Wait, on the last breath, last echo where you move,
Then it shall come, the miracle you sought,
Not in the leaves, nor in your own thought,
Joy will surround you, which you thought had fled,
In safety, in silence, in the steps of the dead.

I Do Not Ask a Gentle Way

I do not ask a gentle way.
Let the road be hard.
Drag or muster all you may
To hinder or retard.
Making opposition strong,
Fit me for the task of song.

No milder teacher than the worst
The athletic body knows.
However hatred, harassed, cursed,
Its balance is repose.
Wrinkled though the outer skin,
A perfect body lies within.

Since the letters first were cut
Moss and grass have grown,
Yet what tenderness is shut
Under every stone.
I proclaim in all I sing
Tenderness the hardest thing.

Villanelle

Time will come round again,
Our lightest joys be just,
If constancy remain.

Though we encounter pain
And winter's ice and frost,
Time will come round again.

The bow that breaks through rain
Will never quite be lost
If constancy remain.

Light has so spun the skein
Of ecstasy and dust,
Time will come round again.

Why should my heart complain
Of distance or distrust
If constancy remain?

Love's voice will not refrain
But tells me, as it must:
Time will come round again
If constancy remain.

Though to Please Man

Though to please man I might
Affect a scornful air
Setting against the night
Strong emblems of despair,
I am too much in debt
To that strong love which cried:
Lay your life down, and set
No store by scorn or pride.
For what were all men's praise
Or worldly recompense
If in the coming days
A dropped voice, more intense
Than any other, said:
I too had solitude
And felt, being clothed and fed,
Nothing but gratitude?
How can I fail to see
That living fountain spill
In equal harmony
Over Assisi's hill
And here, wherever feet
Walk with considerate pace,
No intellect complete
Lacking the hand of grace?

Rarely Published and Unpublished Poems

True Lovers

Look not, friend, into these eyes,
Unless you see twin mysteries
Gleam from out a hollow socket
Laughter fled, for Death will mock it.

Look not up into my face
Unless you see its last disgrace,
Skull and bone and lifeless hair
Emptily foreshadowed there.

Watch me move across the room
As one who studies his own doom;
And read in movement lithe and fresh
The slow corruption of my flesh.

Listen to my voice as to
The cypress swaying over you
Where Death has laid your stiffened limbs;
And hear my words as dying hymns.

Feel my fingers gently pressed
Against your shoulder, arm or breast
Mortally; and hear my breath
Sighing like the wind of Death.

But question not the apocalypse
Shaped by the utterance of these lips,
Nor ask the wisdom of the waves
Why flowers bloom on barren graves.

Through Regret and through Remorse
True lovers find a lover's corse,
And in the winding-sheet, more scope
Than Life gave, for immortal hope.

from *Sonnets of Resurrection*

7

Father of light, to whom the innumerable
Doomed, single-fated being adoring prays,
No two souls bound can strengthen one soul's praise,
The shout fresh-risen from the leper's well.
To robust men, to lives healthy and well
I lift no gratitude in the course of days,
But to Him only who in a night could raise
Miraculous life from miracle-murdering hell.
For I have seen, beyond the counselling stones
Of grains and houses, pitched by utmost thought
Beyond time's chain, preying on that righteous dreamer,
In the black hour that cast salvation out,
Love snatch me, a miracle, from the trough of groans
To the infinite, suffering love of my great Redeemer.

Untitled

Every creation of love has a twofold certainty,
Spirit begotten of spirit, flesh of flesh
And every moment of life, however trivial,
Is pursued by the snake-headed girls, and acclaimed by legions
of angels.

Slender, beautiful trumpets raised by the rounded mouths
Of ecstatic worshippers; marvellous music of silence;
In the Lorenzkirche the suspended flight of angels;
The columns of stone; the slanting light; the breath of dumb names.

When I count the poets I love, each has a moment of terror,
The rest of his life is a fiction. Time has no part in the work.
To have heard the terrible cymbals, to have been in that presence
Once, was sufficient to blast time out. Then a nymph cried softly:

Return to the natural river of childhood. For you I have waited,
Creature of many exiles,
Who trust the tip of the flame,
Innocence, father of intellect, light upon water playing.

Parable Winkle

Parable winkle
Slipped from a crinkle,
Dropped through the seaweed brown and wet.
Down came the Tashai,
Flish-eye, flash-eye,
Caught him in the bottom of his bamboo net.

Limpet and mussel
Tugged in a tussle,
Tightening their grip on the slippery slab,
Fearing the Tashai,
Flish-eye, flash-eye,
Greater in his grapple than the green-eyed crab.

'Flish-eye, Flash-eye,
Flish-eye, Flash-eye,
Prop me on top where I want to be,
Not in that coolie
Pearly pooly,
Spangled with the tangles of the gulping sea.'

'No: I shall find you
First, then wind you
Out of your oil-bright coils within;
Boiled, I shall bring you,
Prong you, pring you,
Proffered in the open on a palace pin.'

Parable winkle
Then in a twinkle
Saw the glint of his half-shut eye,
Slipped as he scooped him,
Scuttled and escaped him,
Leaving only bubbles in the bamboo sky.

Attis

Voices. Voices.
He it was told me to find my way to the stones.
The stones will tell me, he said. The stones. The stones.
How terribly still they are. Is there one among them
Can answer? The rocks have echoes. All the world's ways I moved
Distrusting language. Lovers of the seasons came,
But I clung to the fountain of dust. Dust, I said,
The hills have beautiful stories, but there are no rivers
That do not flow down to you; you hold the single voice
That has shaken my soul, a still, a terrible voice.
Then the women passed, with pitchers of music, turned
A moment in sunlight, smiled.
Dust, I said,
Though they look beautiful, you have a subtler beauty.
This thing is sure:
The seasons will be annihilated.
Your beauty is under the seasons.
And where I stood the seasons whirled on my heel,
As I said this saying to the listening wind, aloud.

So I asked one man, he was blind, they called him Tiresias,
The sage in the rocks of the hills where I followed my sheep,
A boy looking forward. I said: There are veils on my eyes,
But I will not follow the pattern those masters have painted.
Tear them away.
Tell me the way to the sea.

So I came.
And I wound through the gorges where the rocks hover like eagles,
Under the rocks that hover like eagles,
And every step I took the talons were nearer.
I was already the lives of all lovers. I knew it.
In a breath Adonis, in a breath Prometheus. My breathing
Devoured the mountains; the world swam into my nakedness.
You will take all from me, I said, speaking to no man,
But you will not take this voice.
No, nor its pledge to the dust.
It is more ancient than you.
I can face you, O sun,
My light is behind you. And, winds, you carry away
Nothing I seek. My breath is under your movement.
Then I turned to the silence beside me, walking like a companion.
I turned and I said, Come nearer.
Come nearer: we are alone.
Terrible spirit, I said, no two can come
So near as we are this moment.
Though I do not see you, I know you in every fibre
Of my body. Nor can two tell
How many invisible natures
Support the visible arm.
I spoke, and the tongue was mine, yet the words were another's;
That voice had come from the bone.

I passed within the waterfall
Thundering eternally. Wings and the movement of wings
Shone and sounded in light,
A thousand commingled birds, and one that was silent,
A thousand commingled sounds, and one that was silent.
Unending music, unending, descending, moving
In a trance of rainbows and aeons,
Looms of light and sound, death-dealing, miraculous looms.
I said, I have broken those looms for I have eluded them.
I know the years, the seasons and centuries are a vapour.
I have followed a secret course,
A course like the course of music,
And the beautiful order of stars is alive in my wrist.
I looked to the ground.

I looked.
There was blood on the cyclamen.

Then out of the caves
Sprang Love's worshippers. I saw them riding on clouds.
The sky rained blood on my eyes. In the sight of Love's limbs
The tongue is powerless. Spellbound I followed
The ritual of blood, the procession of magical beasts,
The music of horns and trumpets, strident shrieking,
Clashing of tribal cymbals,
Men like gods, shooting like a comet, women in their embraces,
Illuminating the clouds,
Diving and rising in light, scattering enamoured drops,
Trampling the lewd vibration of bells, possessing each other,
And around me was burning, ritual dancing, and burning,
Burning and music, the massacre of the virgins,
Vanishing and returning
In the shower of regeneration, the rain of Earth's blood.

Goaded out of their sight by the tridents and scourges
Of the sea-gods and Furies protecting the tender embrace,
I left the orgiastic, eruptive mountain,
My eyes fixed on the dust, remembering the words of Tiresias:
Stand but a moment longer, a breath will suffice
If you hold all ages fast in the faith of your pulse,
To break the delusion of dust.
And the mounting midnight bull
And circling horses and dolphins mocked my erroneous shadow,
But I murmured: Stay near me, Tiresias,
You know that none is so passionate
As he whose love is doomed in an ageless lifetime
To mate with the breathless dust.
Then the rites receded, spun back from my waking footprint;
And I journeyed through the seasons and lives to the thought of
death;
Then I knew that none is so passionate.
So I came at last to the stones.

The Melodramatic

At most the melodramatic
Is less than half of a man.
A farthing would make his attic
Ring like an empty can.

After the crucifixion
Whose every nail is fact,
Who could believe the fiction
Of a melodramatic act?

The brag, the colourful caper,
Is a shabby substitute
For the demands of paper
And the strict notes of the flute.

Forever picking a quarrel,
He tastes the fruit of the sloe
And envies the brighter laurel,
And knows not where to go.

His indignation's a rudder
Caught in a tangle of kelp.
His cries of remorse and murder
Are the drowner's cry for help.

He sees his body as broken
And cast up on a beach
Where it points to a truth unspoken
Which reason could not reach.

And yet the melodramatic
Does the true creature wrong.
Silence is more emphatic,
A stricter teacher of song.

Aphorisms

Natural speech may be excellent, but who will remember it unless it is allied to something artificial, to a particular order of music?

Criticism projects its high tone, its flattering responses, but of what man-made echo does the mind not weary, as it turns endlessly round the Earth?

Ambition is wholly imitative and wholly competitive until it has died.

Unredeemed ambition is the desire to survive the present. Its direction is despair.

Redeemed ambition is the willingness to die rather than accept a survival alien to present truth. Its direction is compassion.

Religious poetry is sealed like the eyes of Lazarus by a refusal to be raised except by the true God.

The fountain, what is it? What is ancient, what is fresh.

Defects of the imagination are always reflected in style.

Vagueness is an enemy of holiness; the soul of harmony continually thirsts for definition.

The epic depends on exactness of detail: the larger the theme, the more minute its organisation.

The syllable is the strictest instructor. For the lyric poet what better critic than silence?

A poet need have only one enemy: his reputation.

Write for the dead, if you will not disappoint the living.

The stammerer may arrive at the truth the fluent speaker missed.

A true style cannot be learnt from contemporaries.

A fragmentary statement of truth is better than a polished falsification, for how could that live, even for a moment, beside what is eternally fresh?

What is revision except, in the interests of unity, to eliminate the evidence of words?

Suffering is a great teacher: we know nothing until we know that.

Lyrical poetry at its best is the physical body of what the imagination recognises as truth.

The point of balance in a poem is unpredictable. Whatever weight a poet brings to it, beyond a certain point the poem writes itself.

Composition is spontaneous, but true spontaneity in poetry is nearly always a delayed thing. It is the check, the correction, the transfigured statement, that makes the poem unforgettable.

A poet, overhearing a conversation out of time, must be his time's interpreter; but how can the Muse know this, whose eyes are fixed on what is eternally fresh and continually beginning?

Critics, even unimportant ones, are bound to demonstrate their vitality, like sandhoppers.

The true critic, the true discoverer, stays in the same place.

A true poem renews itself at its close.

Art is miraculous. There is no destructive or restrictive theory of art which cannot be contradicted by a work of genius.

Notes

The dates given are the final dates for poems, often much later than those of the first drafts: 'True spontaneity, true art, seems to me to come, more often than not, long after the poem's first conception' ('The Second Pressure in Poetry', *Unicorn 10*, Spring 1963).

The Ballad of the Mari Lwyd (1941)
The forty-one poems of Watkins's first volume were written between 1934 and 1941. After Watkins's transformatory experience of 1928, he had destroyed or repudiated his earlier poems, 'and there must have been a thousand'. He did not see fit to publish the poetry he wrote between 1928 and 1934, partly because: 'It took me several years for my style to catch up with this experience' (*Poetry and Experience*). The poems of *The Ballad of the Mari Lwyd* are therefore by no means Watkins's earliest poems, but represent the first poems he recognised as stemming from his authentic, poetic voice. While with the RAF, in 1942, he wrote to Peter Hellings: 'It takes ages to find a tongue. Mine has been locked or torn out here, but I know what it is, and even years of silence are less than a breath between one utterance.'

'The Collier' (1938)
The poem Watkins placed first in his first book, possibly because of its autobiographical resonances. Its opening resounds with Watkins's own birth in the midst of a rare earthquake in the coalmining region of South Wales.

In Nuremberg, aged twenty-four, Watkins had witnessed a performance of 'the *Josephslegende* of Strauss; a work of immortal beauty and most wonderfully portrayed. It... shows the pagan rule of tyranny, savagery, lust and monarchical pride penetrated by the subtle spirit of free untamed aesthetic beauty evolved from innocent childhood in the figure of Joseph' (Notebook, 9 June 1931, National Library of Wales (NLW) Manuscript 22447B).

'Griefs of the Sea' (1937)
The very first poem Watkins offered for publication after renouncing his earlier decision not to publish. The poem marks the beginning, in many ways, of Watkins's true poetic voice. He spoke in a letter of '*Griefs of the Sea*, which I *heard* coming out of the grass of the cliffs of Pennard and Hunt's Bay' (Letter to F. Dufau-Labeyrie in *Temenos 8*).

'Stone Footing' (1940)
The poem relates, clearly, to Watkins's self-chosen poetic path. In an earlier, unpublished poem 'Document of a Live Poet' Watkins wrote:

Examine me. I am the poet, sir,…
How did I fare? I straight will tell you true.
First felt I like an exile from my kind… (Privately owned MS).

'Ballad of the Mari Lwyd' (1939)
'In my long "Ballad of the Mari Lwyd", which means in English Ballad of the Grey Mare, I have attempted to bring dead and living together, on the last night of the year, when the skull of a mare or else a wooden model of a horse's head, was traditionally carried from house to house in Wales by a party of wits and singers demanding food and drink, which they would earn only by succeeding in a rhyming contest with those inside the door. The dead come to the window, and I make them three times as human and cunning and violent as the living. I also show their terrifying thirst, their need of the living, whom they accuse of a total lack of compassion…

'The Ballad had been suggested to me on the last night of 1938 by a broadcast of the ritual of Mari Lwyd from my father's old home in the village of Taff's Well, near Cardiff. I had been working late in Swansea that night, and when I arrived home at a quarter-to-twelve the broadcast was already on. I had a distinct vision, such as one sometimes has when one is tired; and in the next four months I worked at the ballad almost every night. I kept nothing of those hundred pages except the stanza form, and only after another two months did the first verse of the final ballad come to me. The whole poem came, with refrains, in the following winter' (*Poetry and Experience*).

The poet David Wright described the effect the poem had on his generation: 'Watkins's great piece of luck, for which when it came he was well prepared, was "The Ballad of the Mari Lwyd"... For my generation the impact of "The Ballad of the Mari Lwyd" in 1941 was almost as electric as that of Auden's "Paid on Both Sides" had been a decade earlier' (Introduction to *Poetry Wales*, Vol. 12, No. 4, Spring 1977).

The voices of the dead in the poem are indicated by inverted commas.

The Lamp and the Veil (1945)

The Lamp and the Veil, Watkins's second volume, contained three long poems: 'Yeats in Dublin', inspired by Watkins's meeting with Yeats in 1938; 'Sea-Music for my Sister Travelling', a long, visionary poem written for his sister, who was returning by ship from South Africa in war-time (1944); and 'The Broken Sea', 'for my Godchild, Danielle Dufau-Labeyrie, born in Paris, May 1940' (1944).

Of the last of these, Francis King wrote in a review: 'Mr Watkins has felt with peculiar intensity the horror of "the burning of an age"; but the poem does not lack hope. It is a hope which is only attained by passing through despair; it springs from a knowledge of "the truth that abides in tears" – to use one of the poem's most haunting phrases' (*The Listener*, 6 December 1945).

The Lady with the Unicorn (1948)

The forty-eight poems of *The Lady with the Unicorn* are, mainly, shorter lyrics written between 1940 and 1947. All the poems included here were written during the Second World War.

The flyleaf of the original volume stated: 'Mr. Watkins has won his considerable reputation with a minimum of output. We happen to know that he writes a good deal of verse, though he publishes little... It is only with some difficulty that we have persuaded him to publish this selection from the miscellaneous poems which he has written since the publication of *The Ballad of the Mari Lwyd*.'

'Music of Colours: White Blossom'

The first of a series of 'Music of Colours' poems. The synaesthesia of the title well exemplifies Watkins's rare aural, visionary gift. A prose piece of his bears the corresponding title: 'Vision for the Ear'.

This poem 'was suggested in winter by a fall of snow on the sea cliff... I walked out on the cliff and found that the foam of the sea, which had been brilliantly white the previous day, now looked grey' (*Poetry and Experience*).

After Watkins's death, the painter Ceri Richards commemorated his friend in two paintings based on this poem, *Music of Colours: White Blossom* and *Music of Colours: Requiem for a Poet*. The latter is reproduced on the cover of the present volume; on it may be seen the Gower cliffs, white blossom and the 'black swan' of the end of the poem.

'The Feather' (June 1944)
'Written almost at the end of the war after one of my leaves from the Air-Force. I had written elegiac poems for one or two people lost in the war, but in this poem I used only the symbol of a seagull's fallen feather to write about what was lost' ('Introduction to Poems at Neath', NLW MS 22480E).

The Death Bell – Poems and Ballads (1954)
Vernon Watkins's fourth volume, *The Death Bell*, consists of twenty lyrics, eight ballads and, in a section by itself, 'The Death Bell'. *The Death Bell* strikes a new note in Watkins's work. From the first two poems, 'The Strangled Prayer' and 'Time's Deathbed', it is audible that a deepening and intensification of experience has taken place. The title-poem is partly an elegy for his father, who had died in 1949.

'The Ballad of the Rough Sea' (1936)
'The scene ... is laid in the English Channel, the situation is a crisis of fear. The fear is the fear of drowning, and it is the men in a little fishing-boat who experience it. As the sea rises they see a man on the top of a white chalk cliff looking down on them and halfway down the face of the cliff the figure of a buried man emerges, and the aspect of these figures changes with the intensity of their fear. The man on the top of the cliff, who at first had seemed a casual stroller, now becomes the living witness of their death, and even their executioner; while the man halfway down the cliff, who seemed at first an impotent dead man, now becomes their dead witness, with all the power to draw them to death. The two

symbols converge in the terror of the fishermen, who can only offer their own defiance in resistance' (from 'Introduction to Three Ballads'; privately owned MS).

Cypress and Acacia (1959)
Watkins's fifth book contains poems completed between 1947 and 1958. Cypress and acacia are the trees, traditionally, of death and life. After Dylan Thomas's death, in 1953, Watkins's heightened need to unite these two trees led not only to remarkable elegiac poems for Thomas but also to a new strength of poem – such as 'Trust Darkness', 'Good Friday' or 'Great Nights Returning'. It was this strength in Watkins that led David Wright to call him 'one of the very few who have the moral ability to scan the lineaments of our present predicament without turning into a stone, or rattling like a pebble' ('Essay on Vernon Watkins' in *Nimbus*, Vol. 3, No. 1, 1955).

'Three Harps' (1947)
In some notes for a poety reading, Watkins stated that 'Three Harps' may 'best illustrate what I have said about the violent change, the metaphysical leap, in my poetry at the age of twenty-two or three, form one state of consciousness to another' ('A Note on my Poetry', NLW MS 22480E).

'Taliesin and the Spring of Vision' (1952)
'In this poem the three drops of inspiration which traditionally fell on Taliesin are imagined as falling on him in a cave. In my earlier poem "Taliesin in Gower" he was also in a cave when landscape appeared to him not as a material thing but as a vision deriving its renewed life from the mystery of bread and wine on which he meditated in secret' (from 'Introduction to Poems at Neath', NLW MS 2248E).

'A Man with a Field' (1951)
Written about Watkins's 'old landlord, who was for thirty years a musician until he retired to do market-gardening and potter about the field next to my house until his health broke down. He was an extremely independent man, trusting only himself to do the repairs to his own wooden bungalow, which at last he was unable to do. Suddenly one night just before Christmas I found him there sitting

in pitch darkness at the point of death. He was rushed to hospital where he died within an hour. While we waited for an ambulance he fainted and knocked out the oil lamp – he had refused electricity – but recovered and was perfectly sensible when it arrived' (*Poetry and Experience*).

'Hunt's Bay' (1952)
'Hunt's Bay is about a mile from my home. It is one of the rockiest bays on the coast, a crescent, or, at low tide, a dark half-moon of rocks, bounded on either side by steep cliffs and jutting boulders of whitish rock' ('Introduction to Three Ballads').

'Trust Darkness' (August – December 1953)
Begun shortly before Dylan Thomas's final trip to America in November 1953; finished shortly afterwards.

'The Exacting Ghost' (1955)
The poem describes 'the effect on Vernon of a dream about Dylan which came to him in, I think, February or early March of 1954... It caused him great uneasiness, because, unlike most dreams, it had a quality of extreme reality. Every outline appeared solid... He even saw a small mole on the side of the jaw which he did not remember having seen in Dylan's life-time... he was never able to decide whether this was an unusually vivid dream or an actual visit from the dead' (*Dylan Thomas: Portrait of a Friend*, Gwen Watkins, p.166).

'The Curlew' (1956)
Originally formed part of one of Watkins's earliest elegies for Dylan Thomas, 'Elegy for the Latest Dead' (1954).

'The Tributary Seasons' (1955)
This poem won the first Guinness Prize in 1957.

Affinities (1962)
Affinities contains poems completed between 1950 and 1961. Many, though by no means all, of its poems are about poetry and other poets, offering a glimpse into Watkins's own creative processes and sources.

'The Precision of the Wheel' (22 October 1959)
On the night Watkins's first son was born he had completed 'The Lady with the Unicorn', leading to the book bearing that name. Twelve years later, to the day, he received his first copy of *Cypress and Acacia*. The coincidence occasioned this poem.

'Affinities' (1959)
Stanza 8. In a talk to the Poetry Society in 1966, Watkins said of Dylan Thomas: 'His poetry is ancient, as it is always dealing with first things. I remember, after reading my poems at Oxford in 1952, acknowledging my great debt to him. I had introduced the poems briefly and said among other things that a poet cannot learn a true style from a contemporary, and that he must relate himself to ancient and dead poets, and be influenced by those alone. At the end I was challenged and asked to reconcile this statement to my other one about the influence of knowing Dylan Thomas. I said, "Dylan Thomas *is* an ancient poet. He happens to be alive"' (*Poetry Wales*, Vol. 12, No. 4, Spring 1977).

'The Childhood of Hölderlin' (1953)
This nine-part poem, prefaced by a translation from Hölderlin, forms a section of its own within *Affinities*.

'Music of Colours: Dragonfoil and the Furnace of Colours' (1961)
Watkins's third 'Music of Colours' poem. 'One of the most vibrant evocations of summer in English poetry' (John Ackerman, 'Visionary glimpses of eternity', *The New Welsh Review*, No. 28, Spring 1995).

Fidelities (1968)
Fidelities contains sixty-one poems, completed between 1959 and 1967. The volume's flyleaf states: '*Fidelities* was completed by Vernon Watkins shortly before his sudden death in Seattle – where he was Visiting Professor of Poetry at the University of Washington – on 8th October, 1967 at the age of sixty-one.'

'The Sibyl' (1961)
A rare glimpse, perhaps, into Watkins's self-estimation as a poet. Among those who visited Watkins's small house on the cliffs of Gower were Dylan Thomas, Philip Larkin, R.S. Thomas and Pablo Neruda. The last two lines clearly refer to Dylan Thomas.

'Trees in a Town' (1963)
Occasioned by the felling of two chestnut trees outside Lloyds Bank, St Helen's Road, Swansea, where Vernon Watkins worked.

'The Snow Curlew' (January 1963)
Gwen Watkins writes: '"The Snow Curlew" brings full circle the sequence of elegies which began with "The Curlew"'(*Poems for Dylan*, ed. Gwen Watkins).

'To A Shell' (1965)
The last poem about Dylan Thomas included by Watkins in one of his own collections. The 'house facing the sea' is Sea View, Laugharne.

'The Beaver' (1964)
Written after a visit to W.H. Auden in America in 1964.

'Triads' (1962)
The poem with which Watkins concluded his final volume. Some of the earliest Welsh literature was composed in 'Triads'. Watkins said of his links with early Welsh poetry: 'Although I do not often read Aneurin, Taliesin and Llywarch Hen, because I have not learnt enough Welsh, I think their poetry is the finest early poetry in Britain, and unsurpassed, in its kind, since. Even through translation the force of this poetry makes itself clear. I feel the affinity with these poets which does not come from study, or history, but from instinct. Their roots go very deep; their truth is unmistakable' (letter to Meic Stephens, 29 January 1967, NLW MS 22464E).

Uncollected Poems (1969)
Selected and introduced by Kathleen Raine. All except one of the poems are dated 1966 or 1967. The three included here are among the last Watkins wrote.

The Ballad of the Outer Dark (1979)
Poems written between 1944 and 1967. (The title-poem, 'The Ballad of the Outer Dark', not included here, begins where 'The Ballad of the Mari Lwyd' ends, just after midnight.)

'A Dry Prophet' (1967)
Inspired by the character of R.S. Thomas, who stayed with Watkins in Gower, and gave the address at Watkins's Memorial Service.

'Rhadamanthus and the New Soul' (1967)
A conversation between Rhadamanthus, the judge of the dead (Stanzas 1, 3, 5, 7), and a new soul in that realm (Stanzas 2, 4, 6), who has witnessed the horrors of the twentieth century.
    Watkins wrote in his notebook (22 February 1966): '*Rhadamanthus*. All I know is that this is a permanent poem. I can't exhaust its meaning or isolate one completely.'

The Breaking of the Wave (1979)
Most of the poems in this collection are undated.

Rarely Published and Unpublished Poems
'True Lovers' (1926)
Written when Watkins was nineteen, in February 1926, and published in the *London Mercury* in May 1929 – just before his decision no longer to publish.

'Sonnet of Resurrection' (7)
Watkins originally wrote eight 'Sonnets of Resurrection', six of which were published in *The Lady with the Unicorn*: 'Four Sonnets of Resurrection', 'The Sinner' and 'The Necklace of Stones.' This one exists in a single draft in the British Library (BL MS 54159), and has not previously been published. It is one of the very few poems that treats directly of the experience he underwent in 1928/9.

'Untitled'
A single undated draft, previously unpublished; not in a finished form. Probably written in 1956, when Watkins revisited Nuremberg after the war, on a travelling scholarship.

'Parable Winkle' (1964)
First published in *Temenos 8*, London, 1987. An example of Watkins's light verse, sent from America in 1964 to his godson Richard Hamburger, who 'was in hospital for nine months, encased in plaster from his feet to his chest'. Michael Hamburger, Richard's father, wrote: 'To me, Vernon's humanity – attested here

by his wish to console and amuse a child suffering the terrible ordeal of enforced immobility for almost a year in all – is inseparable from his poetic vocation' (*Temenos 8*, p.144).

'Attis'
A single, undated draft. Never previously published.

'The Melodramatic' (August 1967)
One of the last poems Watkins worked on. It is not in a form Watkins would have regarded as final. Never previously published.

'Aphorisms'
First published in exactly this form, but with no title, in *X: A Quarterly* (1960).

Selected Bibliography

The Collected Poems of Vernon Watkins (Golgonooza Press, Ipswich, 1986; paperback, 2000). Reissued in 2005, this contains all seven volumes of poetry Watkins himself prepared for publication and three posthumously collected volumes.

Vernon Watkins – Selected Verse Translations (Enitharmon Press, London, 1977).

Poems for Dylan (Gomer Press, Llandysul, 2003). Includes most of the poems Watkins wrote for and about Dylan Thomas, his *Times* obituary of Thomas, and related prose extracts. Edited by Gwen Watkins.

Dylan Thomas: Letters to Vernon Watkins (Dent/Faber, London, 1957). Edited with an introduction by Vernon Watkins.

David Jones: Letters to Vernon Watkins (University of Wales Press, Cardiff, 1976). Edited by Ruth Pryor.

About Vernon Watkins

Vernon Watkins, 1906–1967 (Faber, London, 1970). Edited by Leslie Norris.

Dylan Thomas: Portrait of a Friend, by Gwen Watkins (Y Lolfa, Talybont, 2005). Explores the friendship between Vernon Watkins and Dylan Thomas.

Defending Ancient Springs, by Kathleen Raine (Golgonooza Press, Ipswich, 1985). Includes the essay 'Vernon Watkins and the Bardic Tradition'. The title of this book is taken from a line in Watkins's poem 'Art and the Ravens'.

Welsh Writing in English, Vol. 8. 2003. Includes 'Swansea's Other Poet: Vernon Watkins and The Threshold between Worlds' by Rowan Williams.

A Bibliographical Guide to Twenty-Four Modern Anglo-Welsh Writers, John Harris (Cardiff University of Wales Press, 1994). Contains complete Vernon Watkins bibliography up to 1994.

Fyfield*Books*

Two millennia of essential classics

The extensive Fyfield*Books* list includes

Djuna Barnes *The Book of Repulsive Women and other poems*
edited by Rebecca Loncraine

Elizabeth Barrett Browning *Selected Poems* edited by Malcolm Hicks

Charles Baudelaire *Complete Poems in French and English*
translated by Walter Martin

Thomas Lovell Beddoes *Death's Jest-Book* edited by Michael Bradshaw

Aphra Behn *Selected Poems*
edited by Malcolm Hicks

Border Ballads: A Selection
edited by James Reed

The Brontë Sisters *Selected Poems*
edited by Stevie Davies

Sir Thomas Browne *Selected Writings*
edited by Claire Preston

Lewis Carroll *Selected Poems*
edited by Keith Silver

Paul Celan *Collected Prose*
translated by Rosmarie Waldrop

Thomas Chatterton *Selected Poems*
edited by Grevel Lindop

John Clare *By Himself*
edited by Eric Robinson and David Powell

Arthur Hugh Clough *Selected Poems*
edited by Shirley Chew

Samuel Taylor Coleridge *Selected Poetry* edited by William Empson and David Pirie

Tristan Corbière *The Centenary Corbière*
in French and English
translated by Val Warner

William Cowper *Selected Poems*
edited by Nick Rhodes

Gabriele d'Annunzio *Halcyon*
translated by J.G. Nichols

John Donne *Selected Letters*
edited by P.M. Oliver

William Dunbar *Selected Poems*
edited by Harriet Harvey Wood

Anne Finch, Countess of Winchilsea *Selected Poems*
edited by Denys Thompson

Ford Madox Ford *Selected Poems*
edited by Max Saunders

John Gay *Selected Poems*
edited by Marcus Walsh

Oliver Goldsmith *Selected Writings*
edited by John Lucas

Robert Herrick *Selected Poems*
edited by David Jesson-Dibley

Victor Hugo *Selected Poetry*
in French and English
translated by Steven Monte

T.E. Hulme *Selected Writings*
edited by Patrick McGuinness

Leigh Hunt *Selected Writings*
edited by David Jesson Dibley

Wyndham Lewis *Collected Poems and Plays* edited by Alan Munton

Charles Lamb *Selected Writings*
edited by J.E. Morpurgo

Lucretius *De Rerum Natura: The Poem on Nature*
translated by C.H. Sisson

John Lyly *Selected Prose and Dramatic Work*
edited by Leah Scragg

Ben Jonson *Epigrams and The Forest*
edited by Richard Dutton

Giacomo Leopardi *The Canti*
with a selection of his prose
translated by J.G. Nichols

Stéphane Mallarmé *For Anatole's Tomb*
in French and English
translated by Patrick McGuinness

Andrew Marvell *Selected Poems*
edited by Bill Hutchings

Charlotte Mew *Collected Poems and Selected Prose*
edited by Val Warner

Michelangelo *Sonnets*
translated by Elizabeth Jennings,
introduction by Michael Ayrton

William Morris *Selected Poems*
edited by Peter Faulkner

John Henry Newman *Selected Writings to 1845*
edited by Albert Radcliffe

Ovid *Amores*
translated by Tom Bishop

Fernando Pessoa *A Centenary Pessoa*
edited by Eugenio Lisboa and L.C.
Taylor, introduction by Octavio Paz

Petrarch *Canzoniere*
translated by J.G. Nichols

Edgar Allan Poe *Poems and Essays on Poetry*
edited by C.H. Sisson

Restoration Bawdy
edited by John Adlard

Rainer Maria Rilke *Sonnets to Orpheus and Letters to a Young Poet*
translated by Stephen Cohn

Christina Rossetti *Selected Poems*
edited by C.H. Sisson

Dante Gabriel Rossetti *Selected Poems and Translations*
edited by Clive Wilmer

Sir Walter Scott *Selected Poems*
edited by James Reed

Sir Philip Sidney *Selected Writings*
edited by Richard Dutton

John Skelton *Selected Poems*
edited by Gerald Hammond

Charlotte Smith *Selected Poems*
edited by Judith Willson

Henry Howard, Earl of Surrey *Selected Poems*
edited by Dennis Keene

Algernon Charles Swinburne *Selected Poems*
edited by L.M. Findlay

Arthur Symons *Selected Writings*
edited by Roger Holdsworth

William Tyndale *Selected Writings*
edited by David Daniell

Oscar Wilde *Selected Poems*
edited by Malcolm Hicks

William Wordsworth *The Earliest Poems* edited by Duncan Wu

Sir Thomas Wyatt *Selected Poems*
edited by Hardiman Scott

For more information, including a full list of Fyfield*Books* and a contents list for each title, and details of how to order the books, visit the Carcanet website at www.carcanet.co.uk or email info@carcanet.co.uk